Assassin's Creed Valhalla Guide - Walkthrough - Tips - Cheats

By Is.Mann

I. Game Guide

Test the diverse trouble settings

In Assassin's Creed: Valhalla you don't just pick one primary trouble level. You can change the trouble level precisely to your capacities and inclinations. This is on the grounds that the game permits you to set the trouble level independently for investigation (for example the capacity to discover an objective or explore effectively), battle (adversaries' solidarity), and secrecy (simplicity of recognition by foes).

On the off chance that you need, you can for example increment the trouble of covertness and make it simpler to find collectibles or complete a given fight. It merits exploring different avenues regarding it on the grounds that the game permits you to change the degree of trouble even after the mission has begun. You can discover more data on the trouble levels page.

Put on the raven's outfit subsequent to vanquishing Rikiwulf

Rikiwulf is the principal fundamental supervisor of the game and the showdown with him is depicted in the part named Bosses. After you manage Rikiwulf you will get the raven family things and it is worth prepare them all right away. This will expand Eivor's base details, as he/she didn't have any exceptional attire things after beginning the game. It is likewise acceptable to improve every one of the things you wear consistently, particularly as it will presumably require some investment before you begin finding or getting other significant outfits.

An extra motivating force to wear components of the raven's outfit is the reward gotten for wearing things from a similar set (the defensive layer extra increments with the deficiency of wellbeing focuses and a more noteworthy possibility of basic hits). At first you get 4 out of 5 bits of raven's outfit. The "missing" fifth component is a head protector you get as a prize for overcoming the subsequent principle chief – Kjotve.

Attempt to arrive at Power 20 preceding going to England

As an update, Power is a factor showing how solid the legend is. You can build this boundary essentially by updating your character to the following experience levels and allocating the gained aptitude focuses to open new abilities from the advancement tree. Entering a locale with too ground-breaking foes implies major issues – adversaries will be more hard to overcome and will do bargain substantially more harm.

Attempt to arrive at Power 20 preceding you leave Norway and go to England unexpectedly. The initial two areas in England are suggested for Power 20 characters. You can accomplish this incentive by finishing primary missions as well as side exercises, for example, occasions or discovering mysteries during the main hours of the game. You will discover more data about the depicted mechanics on a different page Suggested Power for a Region.

Utilize Odin's Sight to find adversaries, keys and fortunes

Eivor can utilize Odin's Sight from the earliest starting point of the game and it isn't restricted in any capacity. The exceptional vision mode rotates around filtering the climate for intriguing things. Most importantly, Odin's Sight can be valuable to you for:

Focusing on your adversaries - this permits you to evade them all the more effectively or assault them off guard.

Discovering treasure - in the event that you don't see the fortune in spite of the images on the guide (for example the yellow dab) move the camera vertically - it tends to be on the top of a structure or under the ground.

Finding the keys - they may lying on display or be conveyed by adversaries. Keys are valuable for opening shut entryways and cartons.

Re-visitation of Gunnar with the discovered ingots

Gunnar is an amicable metalworker - during your stay in Norway you can discover him in the town of Fornburg, and in the wake of moving to England you will be given the required journey of building a hovel for him in the recently settled Viking settlement. Gunnar has the right stuff to improve the nature of Eivor's things, which builds their most extreme number of enhancements and permits them to "introduce" runes.

·Continue getting back to Gunnar with the ingots found in the game world, as they are utilized to "money" hardware enhancements (and not silver). Nonetheless, kindly note that ingots come in three assortments. Their fundamental assortment - Carbon Ingot - will just permit the overhaul of strong items to magnificent. In the event that you need to make further quality upgrades, you need to discover more extraordinary ingots. For more data, kindly observe the page Improving your gear.

Occasions permit you to pick up a ton of XP

During the game, you can procure experience focuses differently, with World Events being the second-best xp source after missions. We unequivocally prescribe that you stay up with the latest with all the occasions found on the world guide, just as effectively look for new ones (they may cover up under the blue specks on the guide).

Occasions are various types of little journeys - you may, for instance, be approached to assist with finishing a specific movement, to facilitate a contention, or to locate a missing thing. They are neither troublesome nor long. The game honors you with at any rate 1200xp for finishing the occasion and particularly in the underlying period of the mission it can permit you to arrive at higher experience levels considerably more frequently. Areas of occasions can be found in our reality chart book. We additionally depicted them in the walkthrough control.

Utilize the hood to decrease the danger of identification

Eivor can put on the hood subsequent to choosing it starting from the drop menu (the lower heading key on the cushion), however this is just conceivable if the saint is as of now not battling with anybody. The hood is helpful in "orange" areas, for example areas where rivals can assault Eivor after he draws near to them. It has two principle applications for sneaking around more viably and remaining covered up:

The hood can postpone the identification of Eivor. This is a helpful component, yet know that it doesn't ensure "intangibility". It is as yet valuable while staying away from adversaries at a medium distance.

The hood may permit mixing in with the environmental factors. For instance, Eivor can sit on a seat or stop at a table permitting him/her to cover up. For this situation, you don't need to stress over keeping a protected distance, yet the drawback of this arrangement is the need to remain still. So this is essentially helpful on the off chance that you are sitting tight for a mission objective or some other occasion.

Utilize the materials for the main overhauls of proportions and quiver.

In the game, you can spend making materials to improve your stock. Before you choose to improve your weaponry and protective layer, make two different buys from your stock:

Improve your Rations by burning through 50 bits of calfskin and 100 iron minerals. This will expand the quantity of potential arrangements and potential medicines by 1. You will, obviously, think that its helpful during each troublesome fight. Another proportions update is tragically substantially more costly (140 bits of cowhide, 300 iron metals) and it's smarter to stand by with it.

Improve the quiver by burning through 30 bits of calfskin and 20 iron minerals. You can likewise open another level for 80 bits of calfskin and 50 iron metals immediately or not long after. Redesigning the quiver will permit you to convey more bolts in your stock. This will decrease the danger of debilitating them during battles and you will less frequently need to discover places in the game existence where you can recharge your bolt supply.

Data on the most proficient method to get calfskin, iron mineral, and other crude materials can be found on the different page named Crafting materials.

Make a point to rapidly erect significant structures rapidly in the settlement

Gunnar's metal forger hovel is the main structure in the settlement that must be raised. You have a decision with regards to whether to construct different structures however you should know about the way that you will have an extremely restricted supply of creating materials. Therefore, it is imperative to initially erect structures that will open significant new game mechanics, journeys, and highlights. Our suggestions are:

(What might be compared to the Knights Templar). You will have the option to distinguish the individuals from the Order and chase for them.

Dormitory – Unlock the chance of enlisting jomsvikings. You can enroll other players' Vikings just as permit different players to utilize your subordinates and advantage from it (you should play on the web).

Tracker's Hut – Unlocks the capacity to convey unbelievable creature prizes and opens chasing tasks, which can be remunerated with ingots and runes.

Other prescribed structures to be raised are recorded on the page Best structures of the settlement.

Assaulting the cloisters permits you to secure uncommon materials

To raise the structures recorded in the past area (and all others in the settlement), you need to have exceptional materials. Lamentably, you will never have any abundance of them. The most risky are Raw Materials, as they are not found in huge amounts during a straightforward investigation of the game world.

Attempt to put together attacks on the convents found on the world guide. In each such area, you will discover at any rate two huge compartments concealing crude materials. Striking religious communities will essentially make it simpler for you to raise a couple of beginning structures that don't yet need a lot of crude materials (a normal of 30-45 materials for every structure).

For more data, kindly observe the Raids and Settlement pages in our guide.

There are significant decisions in the game yet there are relatively few of them

Professional killer's Creed Valhalla, similar to AC Odyssey and AC Origins, draws motivation from RPGs and this implies, in addition to other things, that in certain journeys you will settle on troublesome choices. A few choices just marginally change the course of a mission or a solitary discussion, however there are additionally significant decisions in the game that have long haul outcomes. Your choice may, for instance, lead to the obtaining or loss of a likely partner, just as add to opening another finish of the game.

It is ideal to spare the game before every discussion (you can make both manual and speedy recoveries) if there should arise an occurrence of improper conduct or for the most part picking "some unacceptable" exchange choice. Significant decisions are portrayed in more detail in the FAQ area and are additionally remembered for our walkthrough direct.

Utilize the horn to call your allies for help

From the earliest starting point of the game, Eivor has a horn that has two applications – it very well may be utilized to gather boats and to bring group individuals. In the two cases, to utilize the horn, you need to hold down the lower heading key on the cushion and select the suitable thing starting from the drop menu.

The subsequent choice is more valuable. During your remain in an antagonistic area you can gather different Vikings to help. This is especially useful in circumstances where you have fizzled with the secrecy approach and have been distinguished, as you won't need to battle every one of your rivals alone. Notwithstanding, Viking backing can likewise be helpful when you need to make sure about an area quicker. In a gathering you can dispose of adversaries all the more without any problem.

Search for the Books of Knowledge

Notwithstanding opening new aptitudes you can likewise utilize dynamic capacities. These are exceptional battle procedures including the utilization of scuffle and went weapons. With capacities you can, in addition to other things, shoot hails of bolts, toss tomahawks, and charge at adversaries. As capacities are incredible assaults their utilization is restricted – you need to fill the extraordinary adrenaline bar.

The best way to open the new capacity is to locate the connected book of information - they are one of the collectibles type in the game. After you have taken in the capacity, you should add it to the alternate route bar - Eivor can have 4 run and 4 skirmish battle capacities prepared simultaneously.

Eivor - significant pages in the guide

Beneath you will discover a diagram of the relative multitude of most significant pages about Eivor that are presently accessible in our guide. We have talked about such points as the decision of the legend's sexual orientation, Eivor's turn of events, or opening death aptitudes.

Changing the sexual orientation - how and why? - We illuminate, among others, when you can settle on Eivor's sex, is it conceivable to change the sex uninhibitedly, and does the decision of sex influences the game in any capacity.

Improvement and capacity tree - Here you will discover all the data about how to obtain and spend aptitude focuses, and how to utilize Eivor's interesting capacities.

How to open the Hidden Blade? - We clarify when Eivor meets Assassins and access a Hidden Blade.

Capacities - how to open? - This page centers just around the capacities. We educate how to open use them.

What are the best primary abilities? - We have arranged the most valuable abilities that can give Eivor new assaults. They can obviously encourage the game.

Mending - how to reestablish wellbeing? - Read this page to figure out how to reestablish Eivor's wellbeing and what you need for this.

How to open the pony? - Learn when you can get a mount and how to call the pony.

Changing the presence of the character - is it conceivable? - You will figure out how to change Eivor's haircut and facial hair, just as getting a tattoo on their body.

Sentiments - This part records Eivor's accessible love interests. All sentiments in the game are accessible paying little mind to the picked sex.

Sexual orientation and personalisation

Eivor is the head of one of the Viking groups and the primary character of AC Valhalla. You will play as them all through the whole game. The game has a choice to pick the hero's sex. This implies that you can play as a lady or a man while keeping the story sanctioned.

The improvement of the character will influence their appearance.

The game doesn't have a broad character maker - Eivor's outward presentation can't be changed. Among the components that you can customize you will discover haircut, hair tone, war paints and tattoos. The makers made a point to incorporate numerous alternatives to modify the character. You shouldn't have issues with discovering something for you. Furthermore, as the game advances, the legend turns out to be increasingly amazing, which likewise influences their appearance.

Raven and Hidden Blade

Eivor is outfitted with two significant components that make the game simpler - a Hidden Blade and a raven.

Your new fowl companion, Synin, will serve a similar

capacity as the falcon in Assassin's Creed Odyssey. This implies that you can utilize it to scout the region. With its assistance, you will have the option to find foes and significant things.

In AC Valhalla, the Hidden Blade gains in significance. The makers chose to make it to work similarly it did in the more seasoned games from the arrangement. Hence, by and by, it is a savage weapon that can murder most adversaries with one hit. You will get it at the absolute starting point of the experience.

Relationship with the Assassins

Somely, Eivor looks like Edward Kenway from Assassin's Creed Black Flag. They are not a professional killer but rather have associations with this association. At the earliest reference point of the experience, the player will experience its individuals. It will at that point turn out that the objectives of the hero and the Hidden Ones are comparative. The two players will likewise begin collaborating. All things considered, a portion of the British rulers are Templars.

Notwithstanding, the hero thinks minimal about the fraternity itself. Despite the fact that they help it to a limited degree, its objectives stay obscure to them.

Essential data

Drakkar is the name of the Viking transport that you will not long after the game starts, in particular in the wake of overcoming the primary manager Rikiwulf as a feature of the Honor Bound principle journey.

Aside from Eivor, the boat will likewise have its group – the Vikings who will do your requests.

Going by transport has two fundamental capacities:

Arriving at areas isolated by huge water supplies.

Assaulting settlements situated by the water. The game will advise you about the choice to assault a given area when you draw nearer to it. The attacks are depicted in more detail on a different page of the guide.

While going around the game world with Drakkar, you can either actually control the boat or utilize the "autopilot". The boat can naturally go along the coastline (this is valuable when you need to find new territories) and consequently sail towards the current mission objective.

You can build up the sails to move quicker. This choice may not be accessible, for example in the event that you are near the shore or in the event that you are cruising down a thin waterway.

You can gather the Drakkar by utilizing the horn - this is one of the choices on the spiral menu showed by holding down on the d-cushion. This is a valuable element on the off chance that you need to rapidly continue your excursion. There are likewise ports where you can moor the boat, for example to visit a town close to the port.

Group

Eivor is joined by their group. Your Vikings help not exclusively to control the boat, yet can likewise take an interest in fights subsequent to arriving at the land. The game permits you to attack cloisters and other antagonistic areas that are directly close to water.

You can call the Drakkar team for help utilizing the horn. This is extremely valuable, for instance, when you have been seen in a foe area. In the wake of utilizing the horn, the Drakkar's group will arrive at the area where you are and join the battle.

Assemble sleeping enclosure in your settlement to open the alternative to adjust the Drakkar's team. You can:

Make your own Viking that can be enlisted by different

players (you should be on the web).

Discover Jomsvikings made by different players and enlist them to your team by paying them with silver.

Change the group dependent on the Jomsvikings you have.

The changes of the boat's group portrayed above are restorative. They have no effect on the adequacy of the team.

Boat changes

Professional killer's Creed Valhalla permits you to change the presence of your Drakkar transport. You can do this by discovering, accepting, or purchasing plans. To change the boat you need to construct a shipyard in Ravensthorpe. This will open the alternative to change the boat.

All adjustments in the boat's appearance are corrective and don't influence its measurements in any capacity. You can change the outward presentation of the transport and introduce extra adornments on it.

You can likewise go to the in-game store and go through genuine cash (Helix Credits) on corrective things that change the Drakkar's appearance.

Alternate methods of cruising

The Drakkar transport isn't the best way to arrive at areas isolated by water. There are likewise elective strategies:

Swimming - It is more useful if, for instance, you just need to swim down a little stream.

Utilizing more modest boats - You can discover and communicate with them.

Swimming on the pony's back - At first this alternative isn't accessible. You should initially construct a stable in the Viking settlement and afterward pay for preparing to show the legend's mount how to swim.

Spot of activity

Professional killer's Creed Valhalla happens in the ninth century AD. This is a time of extraordinary Viking development in Europe. Inside 100 years, Scandinavian heroes have ravaged spots like London, Paris, and Hamburg. You play as, Eivor, a head of one of the groups who has driven their kin to the shores of the British Isles. After contacting them, the Vikings wind up in the center of a force battle.

Authentic precision

The designers have put a ton of accentuation to make the game verifiably precise. Vikings in the game wear garments elaborately like those ragged by delegates of that country. Regardless of this, a portion of the characters have protective caps with horns, which isn't truly exact.

The game likewise allows you to control a boat – Drakkar. This kind of boat was in fact utilized by the Vikings. They were planned for ocean and stream route.

The arrangement's custom is that it highlights numerous verifiable figures. All through the Assassin's Creed arrangement, players have experienced characters, for example, Caesar Borgia, Leonardo da Vinci, Sultan Suleiman, and Benjamin Franklin.

Alfred The Great, Assassin's Creed Valhalla enemy

This piece of the arrangement likewise includes chronicled characters. Right now, we know one of them. It is King Alfred The Great of Wessex. He is viewed as one of the most conspicuous British leaders of the time. He was basically acclaimed for effectively repulsing Viking assaults. In AC Valhalla, he fills in as the enemy battling your family.

In any case, all things considered, numerous other recorded figures living in the second 50% of the ninth century will likewise show up in AC Valhalla.

History of Beowulf

Beowulf is a hero of a brave sonnet of a similar title. It is one of the most seasoned enduring works of early English writing and depicts the ancient times of Scandinavia. This work was composed around year 1000.

Saint a was brought into the world in the area of the present Sweden and got popular for overcoming the horrendous beast called Grendel and his mom - rivals, who desolated Denmark. Because of his accomplishments, after his re-visitation of his country, Gautland, Beowulf was delegated ruler. The saint managed the land for a very long time, until he defied a monster that was incidentally stirred by one of his subordinates. In spite of the fact that he figured out how to overcome him, he passed on from his wounds.

Beowulf's function in AC Valhalla

There will be a mission in AC Valhalla where you can get a more intensive gander at the Beowulf story delineated previously. Nonetheless, it is selective substance, accessible to players who will have a functioning Season Pass. It's most likely going to be the best way to have contact with that character.

Improvement, expertise trees

The accompanying page of the AC Valhalla manage contains data identified with character improvement and ability trees. You will likewise find out about the three prime examples – Warrior, Assassin and Hunter.

While playing, you gather experience that will permit you to pick up new levels. Alongside this, you will get the capacity to open new abilities or improve your present aptitudes. The engineers tried to add whatever number capacities as could be allowed.

There is an aggregate of three trees dependent on the fighter, professional killer and tracker models. Each has an alternate arrangement of dynamic and inactive capacities. This will permit you to build up the character in various ways. Quite possibly our character's advancement will influence the manner in which the story advances.

Trouble level of investigation

Professional killer's Creed Valhalla permits you to set the trouble level independently for investigation. You can do this unexpectedly when beginning another game, or later in the choices menu. The three primary trouble levels are:

Explorer – the simple trouble

Adventurer – the default typical trouble level

Pathfinder – the high trouble

The trouble level influences how much data the game showcases on the screen to help you discover areas. By picking higher settings you can, for example limit HUD and compass, and diminish the quantity of symbols showing up on the world guide.

Notwithstanding the chose trouble level, you can likewise empower/incapacitate the distance and closest action symbols.

It is important here that regardless of whether you don't change the default trouble level during the game, the game may compel you to search for something identified with a specific journey with no assistance.

In the later locales, an ever increasing number of missions can contain just a printed portrayal of the area that Eivor should reach – its marker may not be noticeable on the world guide. This may imply that you need to dissect the guide to locate the key areas and perspectives recorded in the mission's depiction. Luckily, this pursuit is rarely exceptionally convoluted. You can generally peruse our walkthrough.

Principle lands in AC Valhalla

There are four principle lands accessible in Assassin's Creed Valhalla. Every one of them has a different world guide, and Eivor can go between them openly. Every one of these terrains has remarkable areas, fortunes, missions, and discretionary exercises.

Norway, the Viking land where you start your experience. It comprises of two tremendous areas – you re-visitation of one of them later in the mission.

Anglia is the biggest and most significant guide in the game. It comprises of twelve or so areas and each bigger district is related with a different adventure – a progression of journeys. On the Anglia map, you will likewise discover your Viking settlement – you can create it as the game advances.

Vinland is extra land – you visit it to finish one of the storylines. This guide isn't huge – it will take you probably a few hours to completely investigate it.

Asgard is a legendary land from Nordic folklore. The AC Valhalla's form of Asgard will take you around 10 hours – you can investigate two not extremely broad guides and complete a different adventure.

Fundamentals of investigating the universe of AC Valhalla

Every district in AC Valhalla (with two minor special cases) has a recommended power level. This is counsel with respect to the recommended request of investigating the primary locales. It's certainly not prescribed to visit districts with a recommended power plainly surpassing (30+) Eivor's present force – the saint will have tremendous issues with taking out even conventional rivals.

Fortunately numerous adjoining domains have the equivalent or marginally extraordinary proposed power. This permits you to pick the request for their investigation or cross their outskirts unafraid of unexpectedly being in an extremely hazardous locale.

All unexplored regions are at first covered by the purported. haze of war. And, after its all said and done, when you zoom in the camera, you can see drawings demonstrating you what might be found in a given area (for example town or a nest of an intense creature). This can be a clue on where to go first.

As you travel through the guide, you will see little focuses showing up on the guide – they represent discretionary spots that can be analyzed. These can be riches (brilliant dabs), secrets (blue dabs), or antiquities (white dabs).

Vantage focuses/synchronization focuses, which additionally fill in as quick travel focuses, are useful in finding the world guide and moving from point A to point B quicker. The game imprints them on the guide in any event, when you are far away – you can generally figure out where to go to uncover a huge piece of the guide around the synchronization point.

It is important here that synchronization focuses are not by any means the only accessible quick travel focuses.

You can move far and wide a lot speedier by riding a pony. You will get free admittance to the mount not long after beginning the game. Eivor can call the creature by whistling. The pony will assist you with getting obscure territories you can't access with quick travel.

One of the main things to recall while investigating the world is to try not to tumble from extraordinary statures since they can bargain Eivor harm. Luckily, this is an uncommon reason for death. In any case, you can have a couple of wellbeing focuses left.

The issue portrayed above can be incompletely illuminated

by opening the Breakfall capacity from the aptitude tree. With it, Eivor will consequently perform move in the wake of landing, which can fundamentally diminish the got harm.

AC Valhalla has two mechanics that help you discover objects in the environmental factors. The first is Odin's Sight, which checks the territory around you. From that point forward, you will see for quite a while hints of various tones that may represent, among others, foes, treasures, barricades, sections, or mission goals. This can be useful somewhat.

One of the extraordinary preferences of Odin's Sight is that its utilization is limitless. Actuate it once at regular intervals if, for instance, you are exploring an area with a fortune or an adversary camp and need to try not to miss a rival.

Sending a raven for observation is somewhat less accommodating, albeit still worth utilizing. It tends to be valuable in every one of those circumstances where Odin's Sight has fizzled (because of its restricted reach).

We suggest utilizing the raven mostly for looking through journey related zones quicker (for example to discover the journey's objective), just as to find and stamp adversaries, uncommon crude materials, and different articles lying on display.

While looking for different fortunes, you should know about that:

A few insider facts might be underground or on high retires and galleries. When utilizing Odin's Sight, move the camera vertically to abstain from missing anything.

A few insider facts might be in spots that are bolted. The answer for this issue might be to locate the way in to the entryway (Eivor can't utilize lockpicks) or a feeble divider that can be pulverized.

The game has two alternatives to make it simpler for you to find areas on the guide. You can:

Construct a map maker's cabin in the settlement and purchase counsel with respect to the areas on the guide.

Converse with individuals set apart with a question mark experienced while going around the game world. You can likewise purchase guidance from them.

As we would see it, nonetheless, these are not financially savvy techniques, as these NPCs don't sell guides of the most significant fortunes. The exemption for this is the guides from the game store, for example those bought with Helix Credits cash which you can get for genuine cash. Our reality chart book has guides and depictions, everything being equal.

What happens when you arrive at the edge of the game's reality?

The universe of AC Valhalla has a few constraints and you can't go past every one of the fundamental guides. At the point when you arrive at the edge of the guide, you will see an Animus recreation divider, which will turn you back to the fundamental game zone.

Fortunately the game doesn't impede admittance to zones with high proposed power levels. In the event that you need to face a challenge and investigate them with frail Eivor, you can do that.

Battling - is it compulsory?

Truly, a large number of the battles in AC Valhalla are shockingly required. You won't have the option to complete the entire game by sneaking around and doing deaths with a concealed sharp edge and bow.

The compulsory battles occur basically during numerous primary and side missions. These can be both common faces and bigger conflicts (for example assaults on adversary strongholds) or manager battles.

While creating Eivor, don't zero in just on aptitudes, capacities and runes that support secrecy and deaths. This can cause pointless issues during one of the required battles – you won't have the option to utilize, for example the harm reward to secrecy assaults.

Trouble level of the battles

Professional killer's Creed Valhalla permits you to independently set the trouble level for battles. You can do this unexpectedly when you start another game. The four primary trouble levels for this setting are:

Skald – is the simple trouble

Vikingr – the default typical trouble level

Berserkr – the high trouble level

Drengr – the high trouble level

The trouble level influences mostly the quantity of wellbeing focuses your foes have. They additionally have altered opposition and incurred harm. Not exclusively will it be more enthusiastically to slaughter them, yet it will likewise be simpler for Eivor to bite the dust.

Notwithstanding picking the principle trouble level for the battles, you can likewise go to the choices menu and pick extra settings. One of the significant settings is the pointing partner - you can pick how much the game will help you while pointing the bow.

Assaults

In Assassin's Creed Valhalla, Eivor can utilize light or weighty assaults with skirmish weapons. Weighty assaults bargain more harm, however devour endurance (more about it in one of the accompanying subsections) and can be effectively hindered by foes. Light assaults don't bargain this much harm, however they are quicker and you can undoubtedly do a few of them in succession.

For the most part, we encourage you to begin each battle with at any rate 1 substantial assault. Depend more on light assaults when battling, yet in addition search for occasions to utilize another substantial one - when you have enough endurance and you are certain that your adversary won't have the option to interfere with Eivor.

Eivor can utilize scuffle weapons:

One-gave weapon and shield

Two-gave weapon

Two weapons - the alleged Dual Wielding

It is ideal to test each of the three alternatives and pick the one that is the best for you. The shield and weapon variation offers, as we would like to think, the most secure and most adjusted ongoing interaction. It is significant that regardless of whether you don't have a shield, Eivor will at present have the option to repel assaults.

AC Valhalla additionally allows you to battle with your clench hands. It is typically enacted consequently when, for instance, a given mission or occasion includes vanquishing a rival or a gathering of adversaries without executing them. You can even now utilize solid and quick assaults just as squares.

Intriguing truth - on the off chance that you dispose of the weapon held in the left hand, the principle character will begin utilizing the shrouded sharp edge as a substitution for it. The saint is additionally ready to repel the assaults with the cutting edge.

You can likewise assault adversaries with a bow. We suggest utilizing a light bow or tracker bow, as the hunter bow favors moderate and exact shots, which is more valuable while sneaking and taking out fixed focuses with single precise hits.

When utilizing a bow, it is unquestionably worth to utilize ran capacities, which may permit you to "overpower" foes with bolts, or to utilize fire, unstable or poison bolts. It is likewise valuable to focus on orange feeble focuses on adversaries' bodies. Hitting any such point can incidentally stagger the assaulted adversary.

Other extremely supportive approaches to take out foes are capacities, for example extraordinary assaults enacted by utilizing the adrenaline bar. You can recharge your adrenaline by assaulting, and increment the quantity of adrenaline utilizes by purchasing the correct aptitudes.

One of our #1 capacities is Dive of the Valkyries, which permits Eivor to ascend into the air and afterward hit the foe with incredible power. You can open this capacity by visiting the Isle of Ely Monastery in the Grantebridgescire locale in Anglia.

In certain fights, you can be joined by partners – they can make the battles a lot simpler, as most rivals won't be centered around Eivor. Search for the occasion to assault foes zeroed in on battling another person from the back. This is especially helpful in the event that you have runes that award reward harm to back assaults.

Aside from standard foes, you can likewise confront tip top forms – you will remember them by the names showed over their heads and diverse looking wellbeing bars.

The strategies of battling these adversaries don't vary fundamentally, despite the fact that you should know that they won't be vanquished so rapidly. Attempt to drain their protection bar to open them to more grounded assaults. You can likewise attempt to debilitate them before the real battle begins by sneaking up on them from behind and utilizing the concealed sharp edge. World class rivals utilize red assaults all the more regularly, so watch their endurance and respond to these unblockable assaults.

Guard and mending

You can safeguard yourself against foe assaults in a few unique manners. Avoids and rolls are unquestionably the most helpful. By and large, evades (press the catch once) should sufficiently be to spare Eivor from accepting harm. The moves (hold the key) are helpful in circumstances where the adversary will utilize a more grounded long-range assault and you need to keep away from it.

Brush With Death capacity is related with evades. It can slow time consequently in the event that you keep away from an assault ultimately. It is an incredible method mostly for battling supervisors. In the wake of initiating the moderate movement, you can interfere with your rival's assault and go into the hostile (ideally by utilizing a solid assault).

Other viable protection methods are impeding and repelling assaults. The last is unquestionably additionally intriguing, despite the fact that it requires wonderful planning – the square catch should be squeezed (not held!) when the adversary's assault is going to arrive at Eivor. You need to rehearse this move a ton – on the off chance that you miss, the legend can be hit.

Effective repel can take your adversary out of adjust and permit you to counterattack. The significant data, in any case, is that you can't repel or obstruct the red assaults. The main thing you can do is to evade (or ideally a roll if the red assault has a long reach).

Attempt to consistently have whatever number proportions as would be prudent. This will permit you to recuperate Eivor's injuries. This is significant in light of the fact that as a matter of course the wellbeing bar can't recover itself.

Subsequent to spending all the apportions, you can either get away or search for mushrooms/shrubberies to rapidly mend yourself.

More data about reestablishing Eivor to full wellbeing can be found on the Treatment page in the FAQ section.

In AC Valhalla, you can likewise get ready for more troublesome battles by holding feasts in the settlement. Eivor would thus be able to get a 3-hour buff/reward to insights, for example longer wellbeing or endurance bars. This theme is examined in more detail in the Settlement section.

Eivor's endurance and foe safeguard bars

Attempt to notice your endurance bar situated under Eivor's wellbeing bar. In the event that you run out of endurance, you won't have the option to evade or hinder temporarily. This can push you into genuine difficulty, particularly in the event that it is a battle against a chief and they are going to utilize their most grounded assaults.

You exhaust endurance by doing moves, blocks, and when you miss assaults. Endurance can recover itself. Be that as it may, it will take any longer on the off chance that you have totally drained the bar. Another approach to reestablish it is to assault foes with light assaults – continue utilizing them until you have recuperated enough endurance.

Concerning foes, their endurance is spoken to by the protection bar over their heads. The least demanding approach to dispose of them is to repel their assaults – they can take your adversaries out of equilibrium. An adversary who has lost the entire protection bar, or one of the spaces of a more drawn out safeguard bar, will be shocked briefly. You can utilize this occasion to play out a solid stagger assault/execution – their fundamental adaptations are initiated by squeezing the correct simple stick when you draw near to a paralyzed adversary.

Force, aptitudes and improving stuff

Eivor's adequacy in taking out adversaries is affected not just by how well you are controlling the character yet additionally by how well they are created. This theme can be partitioned into three fundamental gatherings.

The main thing is Eivor's Power – having a powerful level allows you to visit areas with higher proposed power level and face rivals. You increment power by spending expertise focuses in the aptitudes tree. For more data, see Suggested power – I'm not catching it's meaning? page.

These ability focuses permit you to purchase new aptitudes from the expertise tree. These can be new exceptional assaults just as inactive buffs, which permit, for instance, to exact more went harm or broaden Eivor's HP.

We have ordered the aptitudes suggested by us on a different page Best principle abilities. Among the abilities that can be bought nearly at the absolute starting point of the game, the most helpful are Backstab (assaults from behind arrangement more harm), and Stomp (finish koncked-down foes).

The last gathering is the improvement of the hardware, which upgrades our weapons and injects them with extra properties. Notwithstanding the standard enhancements bought with normal making materials, it's additionally beneficial to go to metalworker Gunnar, who will have the option to improve your stuff. This is finished by giving him the correct ingots - more excellent gear can be improved more occasions and can acknowledge more runes that give further rewards. These subjects are talked about in more detail on the pages of Ingots - how to get? also, Runes - how to utilize?

Notwithstanding improving things, attempt to utilize covering components from coordinating sets. This will ensure significantly more rewards to the insights.

Assaults and supervisor battles

In Assassin's Creed Valhalla, you can recognize two discernable sorts of battle. The first of them are assaults, for example assaults on areas set apart on the world guide. In every one of these areas, you can play a major fight. Keep in mind, notwithstanding, that the fundamental motivation behind each attack is to take special making materials, which are put away in huge compartments and which can later be utilized to extend Ravensthorpe.

You don't need to consistently get freed all the foes inside the convent. You simply need to arrive at the proportions (set apart with barrel symbols). This will permit you to finish the attack sooner.

The second novel class are duels with managers and scaled down supervisors – the last cattegory incorporates extremists (solid hired soldiers), Daughters of Lerion and Legendary Animals. Each supervisor has loads of HP and solid protective layers just as one of a kind assaults and aptitudes.

Prior to each duel, ensure that the supervisor's capacity level doesn't fundamentally surpass Eivor's capacity level, since you may have gigantic issues with winning. Additionally, stock-up on proportions and adrenaline. All the most troublesome skirmishes of the game are recorded in the section Bosses.

Fornburg - is it a settlement?

Fornburg isn't the settlement portrayed on this page. It is a town in Norway, which is home to Eivor and his kindred Vikings. You visit Fornburg unexpectedly not long after beginning of the game. It offers numerous fundamental exercises (for example metal forger hovel, trader, little games). Nonetheless, Fornburg can't be created in any capacity.

It is important that even after the Vikings set off to overcome England Fornburg won't unexpectedly get inaccessible. The game permits you to re-visitation of Norway and this implies, in addition to other things, the occasion to visit your home town once more.

How to open admittance to the settlement?

You will have the option to set up a settlement not long after you show up at England. The legends will arrive at the deserted Ragnarssons' Encampment, which was plundered by Saxon scoundrels. Subsequent to managing hooligans and meeting with the enduring regular people, the Vikings choose to name the settlement Ravensthorpe and make it their beginning stage.

Getting back to the settlement

You can re-visitation of the settlement whenever during the game. This is likewise conceivable gratitude to the quick travel - you can pick the fundamental structure of the settlement or the marina. Returning is particularly fitting after you get the fundamental materials for additional turn of events.

The settlement - advancement and primary highlights

You will get familiar with the improvement of settlement during the Settling Down story mission. You will start it when the settlement is set up. Underneath you will locate the main data regarding this matter:

At first, there are no exceptional structures in the settlement. You need to raise more structures yourself and this will permit you to expand the Renown of the settlement. Opening each progressive position opens new kinds of structures to be raised. At last, the town can arrive at level 6.

A raven can help in discovering raised structures and articles reasonable to be fabricated. After utilizing Raven's Eye View, you can delay the cursor on article symbols and become familiar with them.

You need creating materials to raise more structures in the settlement . This requires Supplies and Raw Materials.

Crude Materials are gotten principally by getting sorted out monastery strikes (attacks are depicted in more detail on a different page). Supplies and crude materials can be found in enormous chests discovered during the assaults. Continuously attempt to open the entirety of the chests with provisions on the religious community premises.

You can likewise get creating materials with another plunder by investigating the game world, yet this is more irksome. As a rule, consistently attempt to assault all monasteries from districts with suggested power lower than Eivor's present force. This will make it simple for you to ransack any such cloister.

The crude materials can likewise be gotten as a prize for making a contract, for example for completing the storyline in one of the locales of the game world.

Pick the structures that are generally helpful for the settlement first. For instance, your first buy should be the Bureau of the Hidden Ones (professional killers), which will open the mechanics of chasing for individuals from the Order of the Ancients. Prescribed structures to purchase for crude materials are recorded on the Best Buildings of the settlement page in the FAQ segment.

More significant level structures for the settlement, lamentably, require the utilization of bigger measures of creating materials. Notwithstanding, here and there it is smarter to assign assets to 1 more valuable more significant level structure than to 2 less helpful lower-level structures.

There are additionally spots for building enhancing objects in the settlement. These can incorporate for instance an enormous sculpture or a well. These developments have no viable application. New ornamental articles can be opened for nothing by discovering collectibles and finishing a few journeys. You can likewise get them with silver after you construct a general store in the repayment or with genuine cash in the game store.

In the focal piece of the settlement, from the earliest starting point, there is an enormous Longhouse building. This structure can basically be utilized as a spot for feasts which can briefly expand the saint's details - more about them in the following subsection.

In the principle working, there is Eivor's room - there you can check the current status of the town (for example data about new structures), snooze bed and read messages.

In one of the rooms of the primary structure, there is a table with the Alliance Map kept up by Randvi. You can utilize it to design coalitions and open new story lines. This is depicted in more detail on a different page of the guide.

Banquet – how and why arrange it?

The dining experience is one of the main special mechanics of the Ravensthorpe settlement. By getting sorted out the dining experiences, you briefly increment Eivor's chosen insights. The details reward/supporter goes on for 3 hours.

They merit facilitating in case you will have some extreme battles sooner rather than later, for example, discretionary managers – Daughters of Lerion, devotees, or incredible creatures. On account of Eivor's expanded details, you will have a lot higher odds of achievement.

You should initially work at any rate one structure in the settlement that concedes a banquet reward – it tends to be a refinery or a bread shop. You can discover about their rewards in the development window. In the model from the image the refinery permits you to broaden Eivor's wellbeing bar by 25.

You start a dining experience by collaborating with the ringer close to the principle working of the settlement. On the off chance that it isn't intuitive, ensure you have at any rate 1 structure with a gala reward or simply gain enough ground in the game.

You need to pay for a blowout with silver, yet it is as yet a wise venture, particularly on the off chance that you have opened more than one reward to the insights.

As we have just referenced, the detail rewards from a banquet keep going for 3 hours (the game stops the counter subsequent to opening a menu or the interruption secreen). The screen shows a little bar of your present reward. Also, you can open the stock move the cursor over the gala symbol to check how long the reward will last.

Professional killer's Creed Valhalla: Bosses - general data, fields

On this page of our manual for AC Valhalla you can discover general data about the managers accessible in the game. In this segment you can discover more, in addition to other things, about manager fields.

As in the past portions of the arrangement, you will likewise run over these kinds of foes in AC Valhalla. Managers are the most grounded rivals you may experience in the game. They have exceptional aptitudes, (for example, sped up development) and battling them will be a test. As on account of most comparative titles, to win these duels you need to locate the rival's shortcomings.

Manager battles happen in shut fields. It implies that you can't flee from the scene during the fight.

Professional killer's Creed Valhalla: Story choices - time limit, outcomes

On this page of the Assassin's Creed Valhalla manage, you will discover data about the story choices made during the game. You will learn, in addition to other things, regardless of whether there is a period limit for settling on a decision and what results they may have.

You can without much of a stretch perceive when you need to settle on a choice. Rather than picking a particular discourse line, you will see data on what you can do right now (for example save somebody's life). There is no time limit - you can consider every option prior to settling on each decision.

The decisions you have affect the course of the game, in spite of the fact that the outcomes are not generally experienced right away. It might occur, for instance, that the character you have spared will hinder you again later in the game.

Flyting

Flyting is one of the additionally fascinating side exercises – it is tied in with offending the other contender. This convention was drilled in England between the fifth and sixteenth century. It is tied in with calling the rival names, regularly in a sonnet design. During such fights in AC Valhalla, you need to pick the right discourse way that will be a reaction to your rival's affront.

To win, you need to pick those that are suitable to the circumstance and are a decent reaction. An extra inconvenience is the way that you have a specific measure of time to pick a proper exchange line. NPC-s keen on Flyting are set apart on the world guide with a venue cover symbol. To begin the Flyting game (aside from the one in Fornburg which fills in as a prologue to the minigame), you should bet some silver. You can secure yourself and play out a quicksave before the minigame begins.

Winning Flyting expands Eivor's charm. This measurement can be utilized for choosing interesting discourse choices/practices during discussions. They may help you in persuading the individual you are conversing with or in finishing a mission in an elective way.

Orlog - dice game

Orlog is a dice smaller than normal game. It's very intricate and learning it well may require some investment. It's a game for two players. There are 19 individuals in the game's reality who can play it - every one of them is set apart with a dice symbol on the guide. The Orlog isn't played for cash however for delight. You can partake in the game the same number of times as you wan't without paying any charges.

At the point when the game beginnings, you can choose up to three God Favors - you will discover more data about them beneath. Every remarkable round of Orlog you win (against another player) is compensated with another God Favor. You can utilize these kindnesses in every single ensuing game.

In Orlog, two players who are tossing dices in turns are confronting one another. There are different images on the sides of the dices. They may speak to assault, safeguard, acquiring a unique token, or taking a token from the adversary. You can choose dices you wish ought to remain and the ones you want to toss again in anticipation of getting an alternate outcome.

It is prescribed to respond to dice cast continuously player. For instance, on the off chance that you see that the rival has left on the field dice with a hatchet symbol, ensure that you will leave dice with a shield symbol that will impede this assault.

A significant piece of the minigame is the likelihood to utilize the purported God Favors. A particular number of tokens is needed to initiate some help. Tokens can be acquired twoly – by leaving dice with red fringes on the field and by utilizing dice that empowers you to take tokens from the other player. Your adversary can likewise utilize comparative stunts – amass tokens and take the ones that are yours.

In Orlog it is critical to design a couple of rounds ahead. Every one of the God Favors has a couple of actuation varieties – you can enact the more grounded ones that require more tokens (in the model appeared in the image they empower you to bargain more harm). You should know that tokens can be taken from you by your adversary. Before the finish of the round you probably won't have enough of them to actuate a Favor.

The "Wellbeing" of the two players is spoken to by stones. Accepting harm from dices with an assault symbol and from God Favors will cause you to lose rocks. The player who is the first to lose every one of his rocks loses the game.

Drinking Games

Drinking games is one of the minigames accessible in AC Valhalla. You can perceive places where you can begin drinking games by the symbols of crossed horns. First such spot can be found in Fornburg in Norway. Different ones can be experienced in different pieces of the domain. Except for the instructional exercise, support in drinking games expects you to bet some silver – you can pick whether you need to chance little, medium or huge number of it. It is a smart thought to spare your advancement prior to beginning the minigame with the goal that you can try not to lose cash on the off chance that you lose.

Drinking games tahe the type of a musicality game.. You principle objective is to squeeze X catch (on PS4/PS5) or A catch (on Xbox One/Series X) at right occasions. The speed of the game will steadily increment. In the event that you commit an error, you will lose a couple of valuable seconds and Eivor will re-visitation of the moderate speed with which he began the game.

The small scale game additionally requires the player to move the simple adhere to one side or to the privilege at whatever point a proper message shows up. This activity will spare Eivor from falling throughout and sitting around.

Fishing

Fishing is another more intricate side movement in AC

Valhalla. Eivor at first doesn't have a casting pole, in spite of the fact that the game hypothetically permits you to fish by hitting the objectives with a bow. It is ideal to purchase swimming exercises for Eivor's pony in the stable in Ravensthorpe. This will empower you to unreservedly move across waters while on the pony and execute fish both by hitting them with bolts or kicking ones that neglected to swim away.

Odin's Sight may assist you with discovering fish. When you prevail with regards to executing fish, you should swim towards them and gather them. At that point they will be added to Eivor's stock.

You should sit tight for opening real fishing mechanics until you fabricate a fishing cabin in the settlement. When that occurs, a casting rod will be consequently added to the stock. You can choose it starting from the drop menu.

You can discover fishing spots all alone or purchase hints about their area from traders. This may be useful in discovering spots with uncommon fish types, particularly in the event that you expect to get the prize for social affair all fish types.

In the wake of projecting the bar, you need to stand by until a fish begins to chomp the lure. At the point when that occurs, you should haul it out of the water. You should control the fishing line's pressure. On the off chance that the strain is excessively high, it will snap and the fish will get away.

Creature chasing

You can chase creatures in Assassins Creed Valhalla since the start of the game. A bow is the best weapon for that, yet in case you're close enough you can likewise take a stab at utilizing scuffle weapons. Slaughtering creatures empowers you to acquire covers up and different assets. It will likewise recharge Eivor's wellbeing.

Prizes got from "normal" creatures have two purposes:

You can store them at offering raised areas found in the game's reality and by doing so pick up free ability focuses.

In the wake of building a tracker's cottage in the settlement, you can exchange stows away and assets for resources like ingots and runes.

In the game, you can likewise locate a couple of incredible creatures. Battling them resembles battling supervisors – they have long wellbeing bars, they can perform solid assaults and is anything but a simple assignment to vanquish them.

You can re-visitation of the tracker's cabin in Ravensthorpe with the incredible creatures prizes. In a similar area you can likewise keep tabs on your development in finding the amazing creatures and gather remarkable compensations for overcoming them. These may incorporate restorative update schematics or the one of a kind bow Petra's Arc (above picture).

Trouble levels - general data

The first occasion when you can pick the trouble level is the point at which you start another game. It is a three-stage measure, as you set the trouble level for the various components of the game independently. This will assist you with changing the interactivity to your own inclinations in the most ideal manner. The three primary classifications for which you pick the trouble are:

Investigation - The settings influence, among others, that it is so natural to discover articles and areas in the game world.

Battle - The settings influence, among others, that it is so natural to overcome foes in direct battles and evade demise.

Covertness - Facilitators incorporate that it is so natural to try not to get recognized and to perform secrecy slaughters.

You can likewise change all trouble level settings during the game. To do this you need to open the interruption menu and go to the Gameplay tab.

Trouble level settings – investigation

The three principle trouble levels for this setting are:

Swashbuckler – the simple trouble

Wayfarer – the default typical trouble level

Pathfinder – the high trouble

Despite the chose trouble level, you can likewise empower/handicap the distance and closest movement symbols showing up on the compass.

The higher the trouble level, the less data is introduced on the screen. You will likewise depend less on the markers on the compass and world guide. You might be keen on this on the off chance that you need to investigate the game world without help from anyone else, with no extra assistance.

Trouble level settings – battle

The four fundamental trouble levels for this setting are:

Skald – is the simple trouble

Vikingr – the default ordinary trouble level

Berserkr – the high trouble level

Drengr – the extremely high trouble level

Notwithstanding the chose trouble level, you can likewise change the focusing on help. The pointing colleague can be helpful particularly when utilizing a bow.

Higher trouble levels influence foes' wellbeing, their obstruction, and the harm they exact.

Trouble level settings – secrecy

The three principle trouble levels for this setting are:

Disciple – the simple trouble

Professional killer – the default typical trouble level

Expert Assassin – the high trouble level

Furthermore, you can empower a Guaranteed Assassination which is enormous assistance. It permits you to murder each adversary with a solitary covertness assault. This can make the game a lot simpler for you, as it disposes of the requirement for unique readiness to murder a more grounded/first class adversary. The designers debilitate utilizing this setting when you are playing the game unexpectedly as it crushes the game's equilibrium.

Expanding the trouble level makes the adversaries' faculties honed – they can spot and uncover the fundamental character quicker. The high trouble level is suggested in the event that you are searching for testing secrecy.

Professional killers Creed Valhalla: Microtransactions and DLC

On this page of the guide you will gain proficiency with the response to the inquiry does Assassins Creed Valhalla has microtransactions and how accomplish they work. You will likewise realize whether the MTX make playing the game simpler.

Truly, AC Valhalla contains microtransactions. All buys are produced using the store. You can open it in the fundamental menu or straightforwardly during the game – you should press the correct bolt on the d-cushion in the respite menu.

At the hour of composing this guide, Assassin's Creed Valhalla doesn't offer any XP helps that would make it simpler to arrive at higher experience levels. Be that as it may, players can make the game simpler by purchasing exceptional defensive layer and weapons, silver (the principle money in the game's reality) and assets utilized for overhauling gear.

Numerous things accessible in the shops are corrective things that don't affect the interactivity in any capacity. You can purchase, for instance, new enhancements for the Viking settlements, abnormal mounts, new examples for the boat utilized when going through the world.

The excellent cash in the game is called Helix Credits. It very well may be purchased for genuine cash. When you progress enough through the fundamental story, you will be granted with 300 Helix Credits.

When perusing the shop, you may experience Ubisoft Connect interesting things. You can purchase or gather them for nothing through the Ubisoft Connect. The cycle is depicted on a different page of this guide.

The primary tabs of the game store are:

Included - Recommended things from the shop. The fundamental screen may likewise incorporate data about current offers and time-restricted offers.

Additional items - After the game is delivered, DLCs to purchase will begin showing up here.

Property - Here you can purchase new artworks for the boat, extraordinary boat enhancements, and different embellishments for the settlement.

Character - You can purchase new tattoo sets for Eivor or one of a kind hardware sets - for instance, a total draugr or berserker set.

Packs - Here you will discover different thing packs. Purchasing a set is less expensive than purchasing single things.

Weapons - You can purchase novel skirmish weapons (one and two-gave), withdraws from.

Associates - You can purchase new mounts and a crow ally for Eivor.

Utilities - You can purchase gold and assets packs. They can be utilized for purchasing new things and updating Eivor's hardware. The game additionally offers treasure maps - the guides can control you to special gear, books of information, antiquities and metal.

Professional killers Creed Valhalla: Daily missions - the Thousand Eyes Guild

On this page of the Guide to Asssasin's Creed Valhalla you will discover data on the most proficient method to connect with the mystery Thousand Eyes Guild, which represents considerable authority in giving agreements and offering extraordinary hardware. We additionally give data on the best way to open every day missions, how to pass them and what prizes are given for managing day by day difficulties.

The Thousand Eyes Guild is just accessible on the off chance that you are on the web. This is on the grounds that every one of its agreements and prizes change day by day by associating with the game workers.

Stand by with them in any event until you have gained your initial pledge through the ground of the mission, for example pass the main mission line in the wake of choosing it from the Covenant Map. Over again tent will show up in the lower part of the Ravensthorpe settlement. Converse with Anglo-Saxon and afterward Reda – you will discover that he is the head of the Thousand Eyes Guild.

Subsequent to doing this, two new fascinating highlights of the game are opened:

You can purchase remarkable and top notch hardware from Reda. These can be for example new weapons and protection components, new tattoos, or new corrective things to be introduced in Ravensthorpe or in your boat. The things in plain view in the store are paid for not with silver, but rather with opals (an assortment of valuable stones). The offer is likewise consistently changed.

You can get contracts – day by day journeys dispatched by The Thousand Eyes Guild. These may incorporate, among others, wiping out adversaries for whom agreements have been given, slaughtering wild creatures, or finding shrouded characters. Agreements are additionally consistently traded for other people. Subsequent to tolerating the get in touch with you have a restricted measure of time to pass it. On the off chance that you don't make it, the agreement will be dropped.

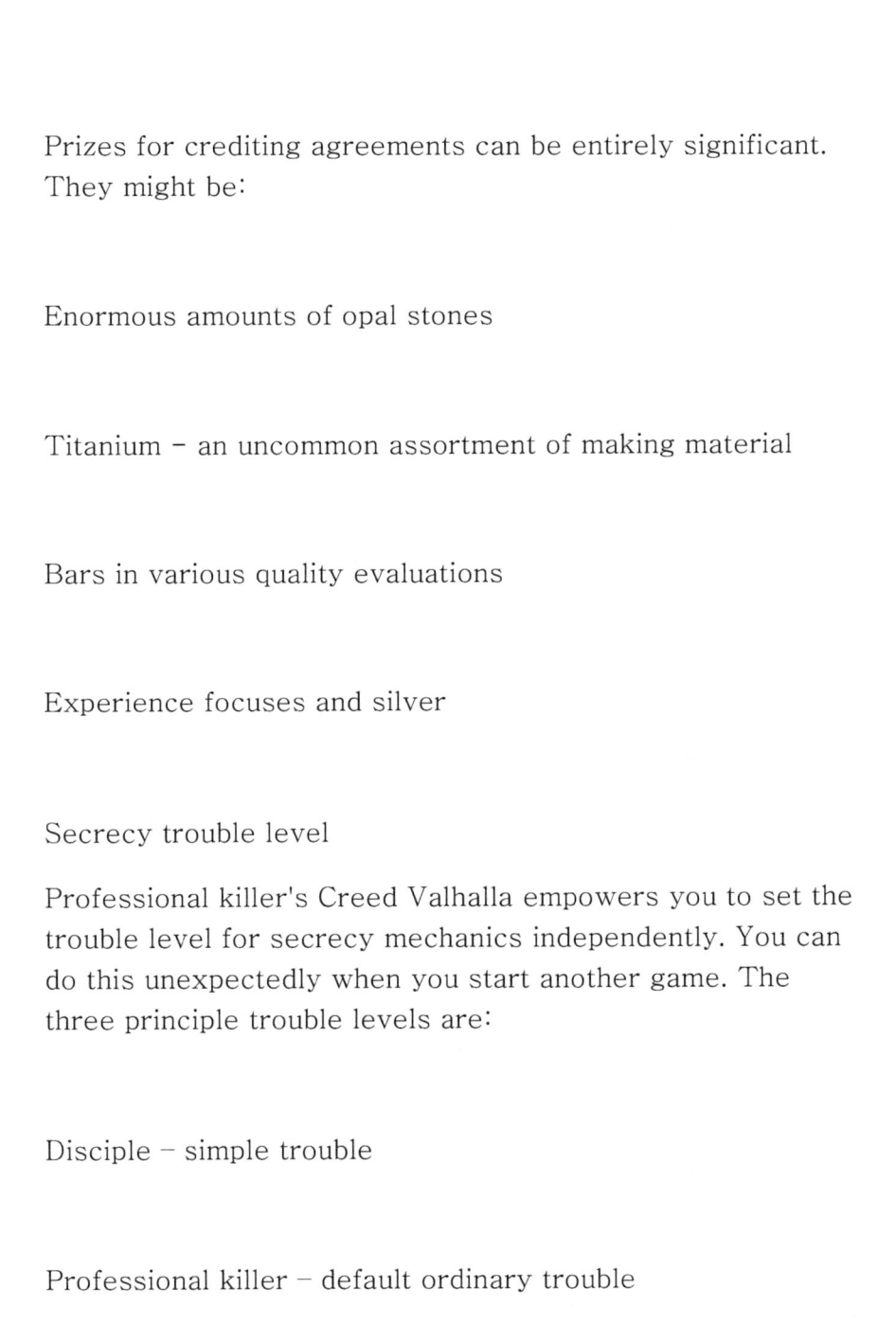

Prizes for crediting agreements can be entirely significant. They might be:

Enormous amounts of opal stones

Titanium - an uncommon assortment of making material

Bars in various quality evaluations

Experience focuses and silver

Secrecy trouble level

Professional killer's Creed Valhalla empowers you to set the trouble level for secrecy mechanics independently. You can do this unexpectedly when you start another game. The three principle trouble levels are:

Disciple - simple trouble

Professional killer - default ordinary trouble

Expert Assassin – high trouble

Changing the trouble level influences how sharp the rivals' faculties are, for example at higher trouble levels they can spot Eivor quicker and respond all the more adequately to occasions in their encompassing. This will make it harder to remain covered up.

You can likewise change the trouble level after the game has begun, from the alternatives menu. The alternatives likewise remember an extremely huge assistance for the type of Guaranteed Assassination. It empowers you slaughter each rival (aside from managers) with a solitary covertness assault. The game, nonetheless, regards this as cheating, in light of the fact that on all standard trouble levels you need to invest more energy to murder first class foes and a solitary concealed sharp edge assault might be deficient.

On our part, we prescribe to play at ordinary secrecy trouble level and, if fundamental, consider bringing down it in areas where it is generally hard to remain covered up.

Nuts and bolts of covertness

There are numerous mechanics accessible on Assassin's Creed Valhalla that can encourage the utilization of covertness choices. One of the most significant is Odin's Sight, which you can use to "filter" a zone. It is additionally an amazing capacity to find and track adversaries. Because of it, you can decrease the danger of being spotted by somebody.

In the event that you will enter an obscure area where there are numerous adversaries, utilizing raven exploring is likewise a smart thought. In this manner you can without much of a stretch know the area of your adversaries, mark them to follow them all the more effectively while controlling Eivor, just as find the principle focus of the mission all the more adequately (for example in the event that there is a particular individual to be wiped out).

You principle device for secrecy slaughters will likely be the concealed sharp edge. The weapon isn't accessible from the earliest starting point of the game, yet you don't need to stand by long to get it – we portrayed it on the page named Hidden Blade – how to open it. The shrouded edge can obviously be utilized differently, while sneaking despite the adversary's good faith, yet additionally, for instance, by hopping down on them.

Another great method of discreetly disposing of adversaries is to utilize the bow. When utilizing the bow, we suggest:

Ensure that your rival's wellbeing bar, in which you point, is completely set apart in red, in light of the fact that really at that time will the hit ensure a kill. Focus on your adversaries' heads, on the off chance that you can.

Utilizing the hunter bow. You can utilize it to point all the more correctly in FPP mode, bargain more harm (particularly basic harm), and subsequent to buying the Guided Arrow aptitude, control the trip of your bolts for much more prominent exactness.

Stowing away in high grass is generally useful in maintaining a strategic distance from recognition while crossing antagonistic areas. You can utilize the grass to evade your foes or to sit tight for watches, just as to drag away individual adversaries. Eivor can whistle and dispose of the adversary who will come to research the commotion.

Another accommodating device for remaining covered up is a hood that can postpone location by foes. This applies chiefly to a wide range of metropolitan areas where, aside from regular people, there might be adversaries. The hood is put on starting from the drop menu and notwithstanding the previously mentioned recognition delay, it empowers you to mix in with your environmental factors – you can, for instance, sit on a seat or begin moving all together of priests. We suggest utilizing the hood in the event that you would prefer not to caution the whole area and, for instance, sneak your way to the mission focus in a public spot without stirring up some dust.

There are three alarm levels in the game. White tone

demonstrates that your activities may have been seen by foes, yet they don't plan to make any strides yet. You can exploit this and attempt to rapidly vanish from their field of vision.

Yellow shading implies that the rivals might be methodology the dubious region. Red shading implies your foes have been alarmed. They will go towards the saint with the goal of murdering him/her, albeit in certain areas somebody may likewise hurry to ring the chime and caution the whole area (you can slaughter that individual rapidly enough or harm the ringer prior).

Twofold death

One of the abilities that are exceptionally useful in quietly wiping out whatever number adversaries as could be expected under the circumstances is Chained Assassination (left lower part of the tree). This expertise empowers you to murder 2 adversaries standing one next to the other in a solitary activity.

To utilize this aptitude you need to sneak up to the primary adversary, start a secrecy assault, turn the camera towards the second close by rival and press the covertness assault button (R1/RB) again to toss the hatchet at the objective. On the off chance that you have done everything accurately, 2 adversaries will kick the bucket and you won't ready the remainder of the region.

Secrecy murders on world class adversaries

Another aptitude that is incredibly useful in secrecy activities is Advanced Assassination (lower part of the tree). On account of this expertise you can endeavor covertness killis on tip top foes, for example those over whose have names and exceptional wellbeing bars showed over their heads. As a matter of course, an assault utilizing the shrouded sharp edge will just deny a first class foe of some wellbeing and you should complete the contend the energetically way. This expertise can dispose of this danger.

You should begin by dispatching a covertness assault by squeezing R1/RB in the wake of getting behind the back or over a first class adversary. In any case, you likewise need to pass a QTE succession accurately, for example press R1/RB again when the sections are in the red fields. Really at that time will Eivor bargain expanded harm and figure out how to kill the world class foe.

Orlog - general principles

Orlog is the smaller than expected game in which uncommon dice are utilized. It's very broad and getting a hang in it might require some investment.

Orlog is a game for two players. In Assassin's Creed Valhalla there is no multiplayer mode, and you need to restrict yourself to playing with man-made consciousness. In any case, Orlog is additionally expected to get an actual delivery (on comparable footing to the Witcher's gwent), so it will likewise be conceivable to play it on table top.

You don't play orlog by wagering your own silver. You can play the same number of rounds as you need without paying anything and losing anything. Nonetheless, in the event that you win, you can seek after a prize, which will be a remarkable new God Favor (more about it later on).

You can pick up to three God Favors when you join each game . In the event that you as of now have multiple Favors, you should pick your top choices, which you utilize frequently.

Each favor has an alternate, special impact. A few kindnesses might be hostile (for example Taking stones/wellbeing endlessly), while others might be cautious or mending (for example recuperation of a portion of the lost stones).

Every special wing in a round of orlog (for example a success with another player) is compensated with another God Favor. The recently opened courtesies can be utilized in all resulting games.

Whoever begins the game is chosen by a coin throw, and you can wager wether it will be heads or tails. On the off chance that you wager the right half of the coin, you will be the first to project the dice. It's important, notwithstanding, that for balance the request for tosses changes in resulting adjusts (inside a similar game).

In Orlog, two players who are tossing dices in turns are confronting one another. The dice utilized in orlog have various symbols. They speak to:

assault - the hatchet

guard against skirmish assault - the head protector

run assault - the bolt

guard against ran assault - the shield

Taking badge of the other player - the hand

Moreover, every one of the recorded images can be encircled by an edge signifying that an extra token can be acquired, and can later be utilized to actuate a God Favor.

Arrangements for the last round inside a given leg last 3 turns. In the first and second turn, you can pick which dice images you need to leave and which you need to project again keeping in mind the desire of scoring an alternate image. In case you will project dice in the third turn also, you need to consider that the images on the dice will be naturally chosen and you won't have the option to roll out any improvements.

It is prescribed to respond to dice cast continuously player. For instance, in the event that you see that the rival has left on the field dice with a hatchet symbol, ensure that you will leave dice with a shield symbol that will obstruct this assault.

One of the main highlights of orlog is the choice to utilize the purported God Favors. To enact them, you need tokens, yet it's rarely a fixed number. An all the more impressive activity associated with the God Favor will require giving up more chips.

The tokens can be acquired twoly:

by leaving on the playing load up dice with fringes – they can be any kind of dice, for example with a hatchet image (skirmish assault) or a shield (safeguard from went assaults) utilizing dice with a hand image to take the other player's tokens.

Note - AI-controlled player can utilize the equivalent "stunts", for example increment the quantity of their tokens with circumscribed dice and take your own tokens.

In Orlog it is essential to design ahead of time. Every God Favor has a few enactment variations - you can initiate more grounded variations that require more tokens (in the model in the image you can do progressively more harm). In any case, you should know that the chips might be taken from you by the other player and that you might not have enough chips toward the finish of the go to connect a Favor.

The "Wellbeing" of the two players is spoken to by stones. Wellbeing focuses can be lost by:

accepting harm from the hatchet dice - harm will possibly happen if the other player doesn't obstruct the assault with a protective cap dice

accepting harm from bolt dice - harm will possibly happen if the other player doesn't impede the assault with a shield dice

because of an effective actuation of hostile God Favor by the other player - the best way to forestall that is to ensure the adversary lacks tokens

In the game, it's conceivable to recover the lost stones through a God Favor - an illustration of some help that permits you to recover wellbeing is appeared in the image. Because of various kindnesses, there are various approaches to restock the stones.

The player who is the first to lose every one of his stones loses the game.

Pragmatic tips - how to win in orlog?

Consider beginning playing orlog by crushing two parts in Norway. The two of them can be found in the beginning area of Rygjafylke - Fornburg and Stavanger. The principal coordinate is constantly treated as an instructional exercise, yet all the others are "not kidding." Players from Norway don't have a "full set" of God Favors and therefore, managing them is acceptable practice prior to confronting more troublesome players from England. It will likewise allow you to acquire the principal helpful God Favor.

Thor's Strike isn't the best God Favor in the game, however it's accessible from the earliest starting point, so it merits figuring out how to play with it immediately; it will beat most starting adversaries effortlessly.

As we get new figures, it's worth to get some assistant courtesies, coordinating our style of play. Our experience shows that the Freyja's Plenty (beat the major part in Eurvicscire) functions admirably, permitting to toss another three dice on the table for 6 tokens, and Freyr's Gift - beat the major part in Lunden), which copies the score of a given kind of dice (those that are generally various on the table). This last kindness can essentially build the quantity of tokens you take, since, in such a case that there are, for instance, 4 hand dice on our side, we can utilize 8 tokens to take a similar number (8) of tokens from the foe. Such cost never leaves you at a misfortune, on the grounds that in Orlog, it's in every case better in the event that you have tokens and the adversary doesn't.

The way to accomplishment in Orlog is to gather tokens that will permit you to profit by a God Favor toward the finish of the relative multitude of turns of a given round. The rival will attempt to do precisely the equivalent, and it is extremely unlikely to truly help it, so the second essential objective of orlog is to get however many chips as could reasonably be expected from the rival's hand. For this reason, we attempt to draw out of the bowl bones with a fringe/outline, just as dice with hand image. In a perfect world, you'll pick bones with a hand and a fringe simultaneously.

In the first round, we generally attempt to gather however many tokens as could be allowed, not stressing over losing our stones. Toward the start of the game and really at that time, it's difficult to utilize the God Favors, so the gathered chips will take care of later, when we utilize more grounded contentions. The general guideline is that in the period of God Favors, we don't utilize more vulnerable renditions of favors. It's smarter to stand by quietly, gather the necessary number of tokens and assault the most grounded renditions of favors we have.

The dice cast is totally irregular, so the game won't generally go our direction. Recall that, and make a point to painstakingly notice the activities of your adversary and get ready counter-contentions. On the off chance that we don't perceive any hands after the cast, we attempt to protect against ordinary assaults (bolt, hatchet) or convey an assault ourselves. This won't dominate the game, yet little blows will assist with making the last progress.

Attempt not set up a safeguard without a valid justification, except if the guard dice have a fringe that yields a token. Stripped shields and head protectors are at last the most futile dice: if the adversary doesn't assault, they're a waste.

In the God Favor stage, you can utilize the tokens that are as yet on the table and it merits recollecting this, in light of the fact that the amount of the tokens may permit you to trigger a beauty in a more grounded form. In the event that the game imprints dynamic Favor choice, it mean's there's sufficient tokens on the table, yet you must be mindful so as not to fizzle, in light of the fact that the game doesn't consider the tokens that we may lose subsequent to gathering dice from the table. As such, it's ideal to check the chips that you have, add the chips that show up as flanked dice and those that you get with a dice with hand, and deduct the chips that your rival will remove – and do it all yourself. This maintains a strategic distance from disagreeable shocks.

Rivals are generally aloof and seldom take any very much idea out actions. Generally speaking, they attempt to pull out whatever number dice with outskirts as could be expected under the circumstances, and they possibly construct assaults when they have a ton of tokens and can exploit the most grounded favors. It's worth to envision and plan for a possible assault by checking what favors the adversary has accessible. We will always be unable to forestall such assaults by and large, yet it's similarly as essential to make up for the misfortunes. It's likewise worth figuring out how to peruse the moves of your opponent. For instance, if the rival just draws hatchet dice out of the bowl, it's sure that they will utilize some help that will expand the intensity of skirmish assault.

In Orlog, it's better not to depend on possibility. We cast dice in three turns, regardless of whether the rival or the player pick all the dice from the bowl in cycle one. In the third turn, we generally get the dice we cast, regardless of the amount we don't care for it.

What number of players are there in the game?

There are 19 distinct players to beat in AC Valhalla - 2 in Norway and 17 in Anglia. Each vanquished remarkable player opens another God Favor, which you can use from thereupon on.

Beaten players are set apart with a tick (model on the image). This implies that you won't pick up a single thing from playing with this character once more.

Winning with all Orlog 19 players from the game world is remunerated with the Orlog Master prize. You can't miss this accomplishment, and on the off chance that you need to play dice, you can just get intrigued by the theme after you've completed the principle story.

All Orlog players - Norway

In Norway, you will meet 2 orlog players:

Player 1 - Fornburg town in the Rygjafylke area

Player 2 - Stavanger town in the Rygjafylke area

All Orlog players - Anglia

In Anglia, you will meet 17 parts in a get-away:

Player 1 - Ravensthorpe settlement

Player 2 - Grantebridgescire area

Player 3 - East Anglia

Player 4 - Lunden area

Player 5 - Oxenefordscire area

Player 6 - Lincolnscire locale

Player 7 - Sciropescire locale

Player 8 - Suthsexe locale

Player 9 - Essexe locale

Player 10 – Cent locale

Player 11 – Ledecestrescire locale

Player 12 – Eurvicscire locale

Player 13 – Jorvik locale

Player 14 – Eurvicscire locale

Player 15 – Glowecestrescire locale

Player 16 – Wincestre locale

Player 17 – Hamtunscire area

How to pick Eivor's sexual orientation?

The activity of Assassin's Creed Valhalla's preface happens quite a long while before the occasions from the fundamental piece of the mission. In the introduction you control youthful Eivor. You should finish the entire preamble, which incorporates getting away from the assaulted town.

You pick sex in the last piece of the introduction. The choice to pick Eivor's sex is clarified in the game by the partition of streams/memory strings and the shakiness of the Animus, which is the gadget used to recover Eivor's recollections.

You can:

Pick Eivor - a man.

Pick Eivor - a lady.

Permit the Animus to choose the sexual orientation - it will be chosen dependent on the current strength of the Animus signal, for example a more grounded male or female memory string. By and large, it very well may be a fascinating decision on the off chance that you don't want to play as a man or lady and if the decision of the hero's sexual orientation is certifiably not a huge issue for you.

Is it conceivable to change the choice with respect to the hero's sex?

Truly, Eivor's decision of sex isn't conclusive. You can change your sexual orientation whenever during the game.

In the interruption menu go to the Quests tab. Press the up key to open the Animus menu. The new window permits you to leave the Animus (re-visitation of this present reality) and Change of Eivor's Appearance (counting sex). You can utilize this alternative for nothing and quite a few times.

Does Eivor's sexual orientation impact the game?

No, the saint's sexual orientation has no effect on the interactivity and it very well may be said that it is just tasteful. The creators needed the game to offer indistinguishable substance paying little mind to the picked sexual orientation of the primary character.

Eivor's sex doesn't influence the sentiment choices. All sentimental relations are accessible whether or not you play as a man or a lady. They likewise have a similar course.

The saint's sexual orientation doesn't impact the journeys. The errands have indistinguishable objectives for those playing either as a man or as a lady.

Male-Eivor and female-Eivor can utilize similar weapons, wear similar outfits, and prepare similar bits of stuff. There are no things of hardware in the game that are simply accessible to a character speaking to a particular sexual orientation.

Character maker - is it included in the game?

No, Assassin's Creed Valhalla has no character maker. You can just choose one of two sexual orientations, for which the game uses two, pre-characterized character models. You won't have the option to change the facial appearance, or the general body constitution of the saint.

You can change your hero's appearance partially getting tattoos and evolving hairdos. From the outset, these administrations are accessible in Fornburg, however you can likewise develop an uncommon structure in Ravensthorpe that will give admittance to them. The game permits to:

Change haircut and the saint's facial hair - You can likewise play uncovered Eivor. The facial hair is just accessible for men.

Get tattoos-You can pick various tattoos for various body parts (for example hands, back, or chest).

Professional killer's Creed Valhalla: Hidden cutting edge – how to open?

Basim and Hytham will be welcome to a welcome dining experience for Sigurd. After the blowout Eivor will get a blessing – the shrouded sharp edge.

The game permits you to quickly "test" the concealed cutting edge – first you will have the option to give various kinds of covertness takedowns a shot the feed fakers, and afterward utilize the shrouded edge to manage the adversaries who sneaked close to the Eivor's town.

Extra note – the concealed sharp edge doesn't ensure moment covertness takedowns in Assassin's Creed Valhalla. The objective can move away alive if:

The adversary's capacity altogether surpasses that of Eivor (skull symbol).

You are attempting to slaughter a world class rival.

The answer for the last issue is to buy the Advanced Assassination ability, which permits you to finish a QTE grouping pointed toward killing a world class target. It is portrayed in more detail in the segment named Stealth.

Professional killer's Creed Valhalla: Abilities - how to open?

Capacities in AC Valhalla are extraordinary dynamic assaults. They can fundamentally help you in battle, for example by shooting hails of bolts at the foes, tossing tomahawks, and in any event, charging at them to toss back the assaulted rival.

The capacity tab is at first imperceptible in the interruption menu, as Eivor doesn't yet have any capacities. New capacities are opened by finding the Books of Knowledge in the game world . These books speak to one class of the collectibles accessible in the game - they can be covered up under the yellow specks on the guide (this tone represents different wealth).

From each book you discover you can learn 1 capacity forced by the writers. You can discover immediately which capacity was opened.

After you find and read the principal book, the Ability tab will show up in the legend's menu. Here are the primary guidelines of utilizing them:

At some random second you can have up to 8 capacities dynamic - 4 zeroing in on Ranged (left piece of the screen) and 4 zeroing in on Melee (right piece of the screen).

Each went and skirmish capacity is doled out to one of the 4 catches on the cushion. The ran capacities are initiated by all the while squeezing the left trigger and the catch to actuate the chose went capacity (for example L2 X). Skirmish battle capacities are initiated by squeezing the correct trigger and the chose capacity key (for example R2 X).

To actuate the capacity, you need adrenaline. The adrenaline bar is charged in battle. Eivor at first has 1 adrenaline opening, however you can open more spaces from the ability tree. This will permit you to utilize your capacities all the more frequently.

Every capacity can be moved up to level 2 to make it all the more remarkable or gain another element (in the model in the image, the second degree of Mark of Death capacity permits to assault more targets). You can do this by finding a second book on a similar capacity. Every one of the capacities in the game is related with 2 books found in various pieces of the game world.

Principle aptitudes – general data

Fundamental Skills are the ones that open new battle procedures. An illustration of the principle expertise is appeared in the above picture – you can remember it by the bigger symbols in the aptitude tree.

On the expertise tree there are likewise Stat Nodes. They don't offer any new methods however just serve to improve chosen Eivor's details. Some rewards have extra prerequisites, for example they possibly work if the legend utilizes the gear from the raven set.

Detail Nodes along with the principle aptitudes are opened utilizing the ability focuses. You can just open those aptitudes on the tree that are associated with the ones you've just opened. Various ways on the tree lead to the principle abilities and you can pick how to contact them.

You can fix your decisions for nothing by utilizing the choice to reset singular abilities or the whole tree. This permits you, for instance, to dispose of abilities that you eventually didn't care for.

The greater part of the expertise tree is at first covered up and just three "beginning" branches are noticeable, zeroing in on scuffle battle, run battle, and secrecy. The leftover abilities are covered up and new branches are found simply after you contact them. In our best abilities list we reveal to you where they are found. You will have the option to spend expertise focuses and go the correct way in the aptitude tree.

Manipulate

You will discover this ability on one of the branches obvious on the expertise tree from the earliest starting point of the game.

Impact: This expertise expands the assault from the back harm. A back assault can likewise daze the foe for a second. The enormous preferred position of this aptitude is that it applies to a wide range of assaults – in direct battle, shooting bolts, and shock assaults from behind. It get considerably more valuable as the harm reward can be set off on more regularly.

Step

You will discover this aptitude on one of the branches noticeable on the expertise tree from the earliest starting point of the game.

Impact: This ability permits you to pulverize the top of a thumped down adversary – you need to move toward him and press the correct simple stick. It is a helpful method to manage adversaries, particularly ordinary foes, who can kick the bucket following this sort of assault. Regardless of whether a more grounded adversary endures a hit to the head, they will at present get a great deal of harm at any rate.

Amazing Attack

You will discover this aptitude in the upper piece of the ability tree.

Impact: This aptitude permits you to bargain more harm with scuffle weapons. The harm reward will be actuated on the off chance that you press the light assault button (R1/RB) while mounting the blow. The following assault will be all the more remarkable. This aptitude "collaborates" well with two-gave weapons, where mounting an assault takes a smidgen additional time.

Light Bow Combo

You will discover this aptitude in the upper-left segment of the expertise tree.

Impact: This aptitude identifies with the utilization of the Light Bow. A progression of fruitful assaults utilizing this bow will permit you to bargain more harm. This reward is particularly valuable when battling gatherings of adversaries and while assaulting more grounded singular foes.

Substantial Dual Wield

You will discover this ability in the upper-left part of the expertise tree.

Impact: This aptitude permits battling with two Heavy Weapons. Of course, battling with two weapons (the supposed Dual Wield) is an option exclusively for lighter sorts of weapons. This is a decent ability on the off chance that you center around hostile form and arrangement extreme harm.

Brush With Death

You will discover this expertise in the left piece of the aptitude tree.

Impact: This expertise permits you to hinder time for a brief timeframe after an avoid made ultimately, for example not long prior to being hit. This is a useful aptitude regardless of whether you are less excited about battling in a fight or like to depend on evading as opposed to repelling. It's important that time eases back down "internationally." Even on the off chance that they were set off by effectively keeping away from the main rival's assault, you can undoubtedly assault the second rival once the stoppage begins. Also, utilizing

Eivor's solid assault in moderate movement mode, you can prevent an adversary from finishing a red assault.

Hunter Bow Combo

You will discover this ability in the left piece of the expertise tree.

Impact: This ability respects utilizing the Predator Bow. A progression of fruitful assaults utilizing this bow will permit you to bargain more harm. This reward will be helpful for managing significantly more harm in went battle. It will be especially useful when battling first class adversaries.

Touchy Corpse

You will discover this ability in the left piece of the expertise tree.

Impact: This aptitude permits you to put a snare on the carcass of a vanquished adversary. After the carcass is spotted and analyzed by a close by foe, the snare will enact itself. You need to set up the snare physically (by squeezing the correct simple stick), yet it doesn't devour any provisions. It's an incredible procedure for making sure about unfriendly areas discreetly. You can without much of a stretch murder extra foes with it.

Guided Arrow

You will discover this expertise in the lower left piece of the ability tree.

Impact: This ability permits you to control the bolts shot from the Predator Bow – press R1/RB subsequent to discharging the bolt. This is useful when you need to hit your rival in the head or one of the feeble orange spots on his body. You can murder adversaries all the more effectively or arrangement a great deal of harm to them.

Chain Assassination

You will discover this expertise in the lower left piece of the aptitude tree.

Impact: This expertise permits you to take out another adversary after a fruitful quiet slaughter. After you have quietly killed the primary foe, Eivor may toss a hatchet at the other rival standing close by, or cut him with the shrouded cutting edge (in the event that he stands sufficiently close). This is useful in areas with watches containing two adversaries. You don't need to drag your foes away individually or thrashing one of them in a customary battle.

Repel Damage

You will discover this aptitude in the upper right segment of the expertise tree.

Impact: This aptitude permits you to bargain extra harm to an adversary after effectively repelling his blow. This can be exceptionally useful in the event that you frequently take part in direct battle and depend on repelling to take foes out of musicality.

Adrenaline Fiend

You will discover this expertise in the upper right part of the ability tree.

Impact: This expertise ensures more harm and quicker assaults if at any rate one adrenaline space is charged. The detriment of this aptitude is that you can't depend on capacities constantly, in light of the fact that then the adrenaline will never be charged. You can lessen the issue halfway by opening more adrenaline spaces and attempting to have at least one openings "flawless".

Crisis Aim

You will discover an aptitude in the correct segment of the ability tree.

Impact: This ability permits you to "connect" the bow crosshair to the adversary who recognized Eivor – you need to hold the left trigger for this. This permits you to shoot quicker to dispose of your rival before he can caution different adversaries in the zone. This strategy will make it simpler for you to remain covered up for more.

Charged Shot

You will discover an expertise in the correct part of the ability tree.

Impact: This expertise permits you to fire two completely energized bolts utilizing the Hunter Bow. The bow assault can't be intruded. This is a helpful element in the event that you frequently assault with the Hunter Bow. You will have the option to bargain more harm.

Last Chance Healing

You will discover this aptitude in the base right segment of the expertise tree.

Impact: This aptitude permits you to spare yourself from

passing on after Eivor loses practically all wellbeing focuses in battle. The time eases back down naturally and you can utilize it to get away, evade further foe assaults, or mend Eivor. You will like this expertise when playing on high trouble levels and when battling more grounded foes.

Progressed Assassination

You will discover this expertise at the base part of the ability tree.

Impact: This aptitude permits you to utilize a shrouded edge to kill first class foes, for example those that can't be slaughtered by a standard concealed sharp edge assault. This is very useful, as it will permit you to execute adversaries that hitherto were just debilitated by the shrouded cutting edge strike. Interestingly, the assault may be effective in the event that you pass the QTE grouping, for example you press the assault button at the correct second. Luckily, regardless of whether you bomb the QTE, the foe will in any case get base harm from the concealed sharp edge.

Breakfall

You will discover this ability at the base part of the aptitude tree.

Impact: This ability permits you to dampen the fall and decline the fall harm by constraining Eivor to roll naturally after arriving at the ground. This will be helpful while investigating the game world, yet additionally in areas where you walk a ton on the tops of tall structures.

Adrenaline Upgrade

You will discover these abilities in various pieces of the aptitude tree.

Activity: Each aptitude bought builds the quantity of accessible adrenaline openings by 1. This essentially implies that you can collect more adrenaline and utilize your adrenaline devouring capacities all the more frequently. Having an enormous adrenaline supply is particularly useful in huge fights and during supervisor battles. Attempt to purchase more redesigns for advancement focuses on a continuous premise to have 4 adrenaline openings prepared.

Run Bash

You will discover this expertise in the upper piece of the aptitude tree.

Impacts: This is an extraordinary ability – we exhort you opened it for a brief timeframe and afterward consider pulling out the point(s) spent on it. The principle reason for opening this expertise is to permit yourself win the A Picture of Grace prize, which constrains you to break 30 items while running. For additional subtleties, see our prize guide.

Professional killer's Creed Valhalla: Runes – how to prepare?

Runes are unique articles that can improve Eivor's stuff – weapons and bits of protection.

Runes can be found mostly during the free investigation of the world – they can be found in chests with plunder. Alternate methods of gaining runes:

Complete journeys and occasions – they can show up as remunerations for certain missions.

Looking through the assortments of crushed first class/interesting foes.

Complete chasing difficulties in the trackers' cabin in the settlement.

Finishing difficulties from the fishing cottage found in the settlement.

Purchase runes from dealers – it is ideal to set up an exchanging point the settlement. More modest runes cost around 100 silver for every 1 piece.

Runes must be put in things that have at any rate one free opening. Fine Quality (most reduced level) things have no openings for runes. You need to discover Superior Quality stuff or higher. It is significant that the higher the quality, the more rune openings will be accessible. This will permit you to put a few unique runes into a solitary thing, along these lines having a few distinctive rewards.

You can build the nature of your things at Gunnar the smithy. Be that as it may, you need to furnish him with the correct sorts of ingot (the most "widely recognized" type is Carbon Ingot). We talked about this in more detail on the Ingot – how to get page.

In the underlying period of the mission, you will just utilize lesser runes, which can be put in any thing that has void openings. In any case, things of higher caliber may should be put in the more elevated level rune spaces. You should get more uncommon runes.

Runes are isolated into those that can be put in defensive layer attachments and those that must be set in weapons. Regardless of whether you locate an ideal weapon rune, you can't put it in any of the openings of your protective layer.

Every rune offers a detail reward – read its depiction to discover what it does and what its worth is (for example 3 to a given boundary). Qualities may change between runes of a similar sort. Check every now and then to check whether you have not discovered a marginally preferable rune over the one you right now have. You can likewise put runes of similar properties in two distinct attachments. The impacts of their activities can add up.

While choosing runes, we suggest searching for those that:

Offer rewards to harm delivered to tip top adversaries.

Offer harm rewards for back assaults – this is particularly helpful while sneaking and disposing of adversaries with deaths.

Offer rewards to basic harm.

Offer rewards to harm brought about by capacities – particularly valuable in the event that you approach certain solid hostile capacities.

Increment the guard of the shield, for example they decrease the harm got.

Increment protection from harm from fire or toxin – you can utilize these sorts of runes in troublesome battles on the off chance that you realize that you will meet foes attempting to set Eivor ablaze or harm you.

The runes can be openly taken off from the attachments. Runes aren't put in the spaces for all time. You can move it to another thing or supplant it with a more helpful one.

You can likewise sell superfluous runes. Visit any shipper (they are set apart with the handbag symbol on the guide) and go to Eivor's stock tab.

Pony and raven

Eivor is joined by a pony and a raven nearly from the earliest starting point of the game.

Eivor can utilize a pony to venture to every part of the game world quicker. It is likewise conceivable to battle without getting off the pony. When riding a horse, you can utilize your bow. Eivor doesn't utilize skirmish weapons riding a horse - can just kick adversaries or wild creatures that are near his mount. It is important that Eivor doesn't utilize a solitary pony all through the game. You can change ponies and obtain new mounts throughout the game.

Raven is utilized only for surveillance. It can discover mysteries, find rivals, or investigate mission related areas.

The game permits you to prepare your pony. To do this you need to fabricate a steady and an aviary in the settlement. To get to the new levels, you need to go through cash (silver - the fundamental money of the game), however the new capacities will most likely prove to be useful. You can:

Show the pony to swim - Not just does it assist you with defeating certain hindrances experienced in the game world (you don't need to swim or utilize the boat so frequently), however it additionally permits you to win the Sea Horse Trophy.

Increment your pony's endurance - This will permit you to jog longer, fundamentally valuable while investigating new areas of the guide.

Grow the pony's wellbeing bar – the danger of the pony's withering during battle is decreased.

You can change the presence of your pony and raven. New skins for the pony and raven can be opened through:

Getting them with silver at the stable and the aviary.

Getting them with Helix credits (genuine cash) in the game store.

As a feature of Ubisoft Connect's unwaveringness program, you can likewise open the Senu falcon, which had a place with Bayek in Assassin 's Creed Origins. It will supplant the "default" raven, however this is simply a corrective component. It costs 60 Units.

During your stay in Asgard, you will utilize an elective mount. This change is absolutely restorative; there's no distinction all things considered.

On the off chance that you own the Ultimate game version or you've bought the Berserker Pack (which costs 1500 Helix Credits in the game store), you can utilize a monster wolf – a mount named Mati.

Wolf

Eivor can likewise befriend a wolf, however this isn't as obvious as on account of the pony and raven.

During one of the visits to Ravensthorpe, Eivor can be met by Knud, a kid who will request his assistance. This starts a side mission called A Little Problem. Arrive at the gathering place with different kids.

As a feature of the A Little Problem mission, you need to execute the hog that holds the key and afterward utilize the way to make the way for a cottage. In the storm cellar of the cabin you will locate a detained wolf. Annihilate or open the confine entryway to free the creature.

Subsequent to going higher up it will turn out that the wolf is agreeable and has inviting goals. You can give the wolf a name – there are three unique ones.

The wolf will go with the characters on their way back to the settlement.

As a prize for finishing the mission you will pick up Man's Best Friend capacity It permits you to bring the wolf and use it to assault adversaries.

You can likewise discover the wolf yourself when visiting the settlement once more. It tends to be found close to the primary structure.

How to recuperate?

The essential method to reestablish wellbeing is to utilize Rations. These are expendable things that reestablish the vast majority of Eivor's wellbeing - you will discover them in numerous spots over the game world. What's more, you can likewise recuperate yourself by eating the food you find. While investigating the guide you will frequently discover developing mushrooms or raspberries, and in the camps you will discover pots with bubbling food. Utilizing such things will quickly reestablish a portion of your wellbeing, and on the off chance that you are not harmed, the food will transform into arrangements and land in your stock.

The most extreme number of put away proportions can be expanded. You should simply to open your stock and pick the choice to improve apportions - you will require making materials.

Naturally, utilizing proportions is finished by utilizing the catches beneath (contingent upon the stage on which you play Assassin's Creed Valhalla. Different catches can be found on a different page of our guide - Controls)

PC	H
PS4 / PS5	✥
Xbox One / Xbox Series S / Xbox Series X	✚

It merits referencing that you will likewise recuperate some wellbeing subsequent to cleaning chased creatures. This isn't the best strategy for recuperating, yet it tends to be helpful on the off chance that you have no different alternatives.

How to reset abilities?

Resetting abilities in Assassin's Creed Valhalla is extremely basic or more all free. You can reset all or one aptitude whenever to recover ability focuses. To do this, open a tree with all the aptitudes, and afterward select the "Reset" choice on the chose expertise or "Reset All Skills" choice. In the principal alternative, you will reset just a single expertise and recuperate one ability point. The exemption is the point at which the reset ability is needed to open other, dependant aptitudes situated above on the tree - for this situation all connected aptitudes will be reset. The subsequent choice, "Reset All Skills", will reset the entirety of Eivor's abilities and reestablish all expertise focuses obtained during the game.

Professional killers Creed Valhalla: Item sets - what right?

The things found in AC Valhalla can emerge out of sets. You can peruse the data about whether and in which set a given thing is remembered for its portrayal or discover it on its card. The model on the screen capture shows a thing from the Huntsman Set.

Each set comprises of 5 bits of stuff - hood, protective cap, breastplate, bracers, and shoes.

The main component of thing sets is that putting on stuff pieces having a place with a similar set opens detail rewards, which are consistently noticeable in the thing's portrayal under its name. From the outset they are dim, which implies they are as yet latent. Changing the reward depiction to white represents that the detail reward is dynamic.

Notwithstanding the picked set, you can generally depend on two detail rewards. The main reward is conceded for utilizing a few things from a similar set. The subsequent reward actuates in the wake of preparing each of the five things from a similar set (model in the screen capture above).

Every thing set is somewhat identified with a particular style of play. For instance, things from the Huntsman set may offer rewards to ran assaults, and Hidden Ones (professional killers – screen capture above) sets for secrecy assaults. As an outcome, it is advantageous to look for, put on, and improve gear components identified with your favored style of play.

Professional killers Creed Valhalla: Equipment – how to overhaul?

Every weapon and article of clothing can be redesigned up to multiple times with creating materials. The quantity of accessible and potential redesigns can be perused by featuring the thing in the stock – these are the square shapes under the primary measurements. In the model over the knife has 6 bought upgrades out of 7 potential at some random time.

To improve the thing with it featured, you need to hold Square (on PS4/PS5) or X (Xbox One/Series). This will, obviously, just be conceivable after all the prerequisites have been met and the potential hindrances depicted underneath have been managed.

Shockingly, it is unimaginable to expect to improve a given thing however much as could be expected at a beginning phase of the game, on the grounds that the game uses two kinds of uncommon constraints that defer the cycle. By and large, it's tied in with improving something very similar all through the game, not just after you get it.

The primary trouble is that the quantity of enhancements permitted at a given time relies upon the nature of the thing:

Fine(lowest) quality - 2 enhancements

Prevalent quality - 4 enhancements

Impeccable quality - 7 enhancements

Legendary (highest) caliber - 10 upgrades

As an update, you can just build the nature of the thing by visiting Gunnar the smithy's in Ravensthorpe, and giving him ingots in the perfect sum and assortment. This subject is portrayed in more detail on the page Ingots - how to secure them?

It is additionally conceivable, obviously, a situation where you've gotten a thing of Superior, Flawless, or Mythical quality. In such a circumstance, the quantity of updates expected to arrive at the greatest will diminish.

The subsequent trouble is that each ensuing improvement is increasingly costly. Most importantly, you need to spend an ever increasing number of normal crude materials – stows away and iron mineral.

More dangerous is the need to spend more extraordinary assortments of materials – textures and titanium ingots. You will begin to discover them in bigger amounts just in later zones, for example those with more elevated levels of intensity. In the event that you are searching for extra data, go to the Crafting Materials – how to get? page of the guide.

Two extra tips:

Attempt to get whatever number creating materials as could be expected under the circumstances, particularly by investigating the game world and opening little plunder boxes.

Above all else, improve those weapons or covering components that will help your Eivor most. For instance, in the event that you like to execute your adversaries with quiet bow assaults, improve your bow to bargain considerably more harm.

Professional killers Creed Valhalla: Charisma - how to/why increment it?

Allure works in AC Valhalla on a comparative premise to numerous other RPGs - a more elevated level of moxy can assist with influence or terrorizing endeavors. This can open elective answers for journeys, occasions or just individual gatherings.

Appeal is expanded by winning Flyting , a rhyme duel that is one of the scaled down games. Each time Eivor's assignment is to pick the appropriate responses that rhyme best with the other individual's assertions. The Flyting begins in spots set apart with the symbols of dramatic veils and we remembered them just for the part about insider facts. You can discover new Flyting "competitors" essentially in towns, towns and huge camps.

Each won Flyting expands Eivor's allure by 1. On the off chance that you lose a Flyting, you can pay to play it again and attempt to pick different answers.

Charm related discourse choices may show up in certain discussions with NPCs. Close to the veil symbol you can find out about the estimation of the mystique needed to utilize the exchange choice.

A more significant level of appeal might be needed to finish certain occasions or to open option conduct variations in journey conversations. In the last case, you might be confronted with the decision of how to accomplish the proposed objective of the discussion – in the model from the image it very well may be a battle, a pay off (silver), or simply an exchange alternative concerning mystique.

We prescribe creating allure at any rate up to 2-3 focuses from the get-go in the game. This will permit you to have a full scope of conduct choices for most gatherings with NPCs.

Overcoming foes

Battle, explicitly executing adversaries, is the fundamental method to get involvement with Assassin's Creed Valhalla. Each murdered adversary will give you a specific number of involvement focuses – relying upon the foe's solidarity. Murdering a standard rival will give you twelve or so focuses, however crushing a tip top adversary (with a name and a novel wellbeing bar) can bring about you getting even a few hundred encounter focuses. In this way, in the event that you need to step up rapidly – center around executing the hardest foes.

World investigation

A similarly successful approach to pick up experience is by investigating the world. Most guide disclosure exercises are compensated with experience focuses. Finding new locales and individual areas, opening uncommon money boxes, or discovering mysteries – through these exercises you will rapidly pick up extra experience focuses.

Finishing journeys

A generally excellent and regular approach to pick up experience is finishing journeys For finishing fundamental missions you will get a ton of involvement, however it is likewise worth to deal with side journey. You will discover them in all settlements, towns, and past them. You get the principle journeys consequently, however you need to begin the side missions yourself – the most effortless approach to discover them is by utilizing the raven and heading for the blue markers.

How to change the character appearance?

You can change the presence of the character in the Tattoo Shop – you will discover it in each settlement (you can likewise assemble it). You can change haircut, hair tone, just as add different tattoos and war paints. Toward the start of the game, you won't gain admittance to this, however you can pick up new components of appearance by discovering diagrams in the game world or by utilizing microtransactions. In the last case, it will be important to utilize the supposed Helix Credits, purchased with genuine cash.

What things can be sold?

The response to the inquiry is basic – there is no choice to sell weapons in the game. Notwithstanding, this doesn't imply that the weapons found a couple of hours age will get pointless. Recollect that you can redesign your protective layer and weapons so they will work better in fight. You can build the combat hardware's details in your gear (you need creating materials for this), and at the produce in the settlement you will expand the nature of things, which empowers you to open progressive weapon levels and increment the quantity of accessible runes.

You can sell the majority of different things found in the game world, be that as it may – runes or different fortunes. You should simply visit a shipper in any settlement. This is one of the approaches to bring in cash in Assassin 's Creed Valhalla.

How to shroud gear?

You can conceal each bit of hardware by opening the stuff window, moving the cursor over the chose bit of gear, and afterward choosing the Hide Gear alternative. Thusly, the chose component (bow, shield, or protection) will be imperceptible during the game. It should be added that pieces of the reinforcement that are imperceptible are as yet influencing your details. Additionally, weapons that are covered up can in any case be utilized.

On account of concealing bits of shield, they won't be noticeable during the game however will in any case function of course. At the point when you shroud a bow, it won't show up on Eivor's back until you press the shoot button (this likewise applies to the shield and different weapons).

In the image over, the bow and shield are covered up. In any case, you should simply press the catch relating to the thing to cause it to show up promptly in Eivor's grasp. At the point when you are finished utilizing it, the thing will become covered up once more.

Opening the pony

The pony is valuable in Assassin's Creed: Valhalla, as there are immense terrains to investigate and it would require some investment to finish this by walking. Eivor can gather the pony from the second he/she arrives at the town of Fornburg. You ought to show up at the town about an hour subsequent to beginning another game. You don't need to progress further in the story or play out any errands identified with getting your first pony.

Gathering/taking a pony

To bring your pony, you need to hold the left course key on the cushion to utilize the stronger whistle alternative. On the off chance that the mount doesn't show up in any case, ensure there is sufficient free space close to Eivor.

You can likewise discover different ponies in the game. The game doesn't in any capacity make it hard to mount them. They can be valuable for example at the point when you need to rapidly begin a pony pursue or escape and don't have any desire to squander significant seconds on gathering your own mount. You can likewise attempt to lose a passing NPC their pony and take the mount.

Subsequent to finishing the underlying missions in Norway, Eivor will go to England with different Vikings. This won't impair you from bringing your pony. The mount is accessible from the earliest starting point of investigating England and you don't need to stress over if the creature figured out how to endure the long excursion. The pony is additionally consistently accessible on the off chance that you have utilized the snappy travel choice to move to another area in the game world.

How to get off the pony?

Getting off the pony isn't exceptionally natural - you need to hold the hover on PS4/PS5 or hold B on Xbox One/Series S/Series X.

A solitary press of the circle/B will make Eivor hunker riding a horse, which is a valuable move on the off chance that you plan to for example hop from the pony onto a passing rival and slaughter them with a concealed edge, for example.

Changing the appearance and preparing the pony

In the Viking settlement in England, you can fabricate Stables and Aviary. This structure opens two additional opportunities for you:

You can purchase ponies with an alternate appearance (just as ravens). This is an absolutely corrective change, as it isn't portrayed by different measurements.

You can pay for preparing mounts. The initial two instructional courses are especially helpful as they show the pony how to swim and build its endurance so you can travel longer at a dash. The second of the previously mentioned enhancements comprises of a few phases. Attempt to open the principal level rapidly.

Professional killer's Creed Valhalla: Norway - would you be able to return?

Norway is the locale of the reality where you will begin your experience in Assassin's Creed Valhalla and where you will spend at any rate the initial not many hours - this relies upon how long you spend on investigating and finishing additional exercises.

After you've finished enough of the principle story, Eivor and different Vikings choose to vanquish England and the activity of the game will move to a totally new region, which is investigated on an altogether new guide. Luckily, the outing to England doesn't obstruct the chance of getting back to Norway. You will have the option to handily re-visitation of regions that you haven't totally analyzed in the start of the game. You will surely need to visit the Hordafylke district in Norway just later in the game since it is proposed to go there just after coming to hifg experience levels. The investigation of Hordafylke with a frail form of Eivor can prompt continuous passings, as a beginner hero won't have the option to adapt to the disposal of experienced adversaries and wild creatures.

Theatlas is utilized to move between the terrains. Start by opening the guide of the current land (for example guides of England). Press Triangle (PS4/PS5) or Y button (Xbox One, Xbox Series S/X) to utilize the map book. The game will show a rundown of accessible principle locales. You can pick

Norway from it and hold down the catch to affirm that you need to go there.

Proposed power - general data

Every district in AC Valhalla has data about its Suggested Power. This can be contrasted with the proposed level of the legend, which should be reached before you choose to go there.

The red shading implies that Eivor's present force is in excess of 30 levels underneath the suggested power for the district. You should stand by and visit that locale in the later piece of the game when your character gets more grounded. In the event that you choose to investigate an area whose force level altogether surpasses the saint's capacity, you need to recollect that:

Eivor will bargain substantially less harm to foes, for example you should assault commonly to slaughter them.

Adversary assaults will bargain Eivor significantly more harm. It is conceivable that a solitary adversary assault will murder the legend or make them near biting the dust.

Extra clues:

Adversaries with considerably more force than the legend are set apart with a red skull. This makes it simpler to see the danger.

On the off chance that you have entered an area that is excessively troublesome, it is ideal to flee or zero in on sneaking around to stay away from struggle.

On the off chance that you need to dispose of your rivals from more grounded areas without expanding Eivor's capacity in advance, us the concealed cutting edge (ideally with opened capacity to execute first class adversaries) and a bow (try to focus on the heads of foes, ideally utilizing a hunter bow).

Eivor's capacity – how to expand it?

Eivor's present force is shown in the Skills tab. It mirrors the quantity of aptitude focuses spent on opening new capacities in the expertise tree (paying little heed to which abilities you got).

Aptitude focuses are for the most part picked up by leveling Eivor up. At the point when you get enough XP and gain another level, you generally get 2 expertise focuses. You can spend it on any expertise you need. This will build Eivor's capacity by 2.

There is likewise an elective method of picking up aptitude focuses – finishing explicit discretionary areas on the world guide. You can:

1) Find Standing Stones and understand puzzles by situating them in the correct manner so you can finish the image utilizing Odin's Sight. Each finished riddle with a stone is worth 1 aptitude point.

2) Find the Cairns and settle the riddles by building a "tower" with the stones. Each finished Cairn puzzle is worth 1 ability point.

3) Deliver endowments to Offering Altars. You might be constrained, for instance, to gather a few prizes from a specific creature animal types. Each set of gifts is worth 1 ability point.

4) Find privileged insights in the Treasures of Britain areas. To finish such an area, you need to locate the principle fortune of that prison. Each fortune is worth 1 ability point.

5) Kill draugr – solid Nordic champions. Each such rival is treated as a chief and you will get 2 expertise focuses for

slaughtering every dragger.

6) Kill Daughters of Lerion - solid champions with otherworldly powers. Each such rival is treated as a chief and you will get 2 ability focuses for executing every Daughter of Lerion.

The elective strategies recorded above consistently give you 1 aptitude point. Check our reality map book to realize where to discover these areas.

Stuff doesn't influence Eivor's capacity, despite the fact that it is depicted by numerous insights. Improving them can, for instance, increment the legend's obstruction and imperativeness, or let you bargain more harm.

To summarize - on the off chance that you need to expand Eivor's capacity, you need to procure expertise focuses and spend them on the aptitude tree.

Professional killer's Creed Valhalla: Dying from the cold - is it conceivable?

Indeed, in AC Valhalla, your character can kick the bucket from the virus. This can happen when your character remains in virus water for a really long time. In the wake of bouncing into cold water, you will see ice impact on the edges of the screen. On the off chance that you don't escape the water quick, your legend will continuously lose wellbeing focuses. Remaining too long in virus water will murder your character. A fundamentally the same as repairman has been utilized in Assassin's Creed Rogue.

You should be particularly cautious while investigating territories in Norway, as these districts are freezing. This is considerably more significant in those areas where you need to jump to snatch some love lying at the base. It merits utilizing Odin's Sight prior to jumping to decide the area of the load. At the point when you plunge, attempt to swim in an orderly fashion towards it.

In Assassin's Creed Valhalla, you don't need to stress over changing Eivor's garments to the climate conditions. You can move openly through winter areas even in those outfits that don't cover a significant part of the legend's body.

How to secure ingots?

You can discover ingots essentially through investigation of the game world. They can be covered up under the yellow specks showing up on the guide, which represent abundance. At the point when you approach the yellow dab it might change to an ingot symbol.

Ingots are put away in enormous chests or can be conveyed by an adversary. Help yourself with Odin's Sight or a raven to find the chest/foe.

A significant snippet of data is that at first, you will just discover Carbon Ingots – the "most normal" ones. The explanation behind this is likely that the creators of the game didn't need it to be conceivable to improve the stock things too soon. Gather however many coal ingots as could be allowed, as every one of them may prove to be useful later.

You will begin to discover nickel and tungsten ingots in enormous chests in districts with higher proposed power levels.

Elective methods of acquiring ingots:

The chasing difficulties – they become accessible subsequent to building the chasing shack in the settlement. You will likely bring prizes from executed creatures.

The fishing difficulties – they become accessible subsequent to building the fishing cabin in the settlement. Your goal is to bring explicit fish species.

How to utilize ingots?

Re-visitation of metalworker Gunnar with all the ingots. At first, he will remain in the town of Fornburg in Norway, however later he will go to England along with the hero and different Vikings. You will get the primary journey of building a smithy's hovel in Ravensthorpe.

Ingots are utilized to overhaul your stuff:

Carbon Ingot - an object of fine quality is improved to prevalent quality

Nickel Ingot - an object of better quality is improved than perfect quality

Tungsten Ingot - an object of faultless quality is improved to the legendary quality

Contingent upon the thing, each redesign can devour from 1 to a few ingots.

Improving the stuff quality includes three sorts of rewards:

Thenumber of allowed thing redesigns is expanded. This is represented by the square shapes noticeable under the thing insights - in the model from the image, expanding the nature of the hatchet can build the quantity of upgrades from 2 to 4. Every improvement burns-through making materials and raises the measurements of the thing.

Spaces for runes show up. Subsequent to setting the runes in the opening they may expand its details or gain some new highlights.

The presence of the article changes marginally.

Cowhide

This material can be acquired most effectively by executing creatures and cooperating with their bodies to skin them. The significant news, for this situation, is that you don't need to chase just wild creatures. You can likewise get cowhide by executing livestock, for example, sheep or pigs. The upside of this technique is that you won't be assaulted by them.

Alternate approaches to acquire calfskin are to discover them along with another plunder (for example in chests) and getting them from sellers.

Iron metal

This material can be most effectively gotten by decimating obsidian stones found in the game world. An illustration of an obsidian stone is appeared in the above screen capture. Obliterating the stone doesn't consequently yield crude materials – press the connection key to gather them starting from the earliest stage.

Alternate approaches to get iron metal incorporate thinking that its along with another plunder (for example in chests) and getting them from merchants.

Texture/Titanium Ingot/Opal

These are uncommon varieties of materials that you can basically discover through the investigation of the game world. Make sure to utilize Odin's Sight to find intelligent items inside your environmental factors.

You can likewise acquire opal and titanium ingots in an alternate manner – get them as a prize for playing out the undertakings of the Thousand Eyes society. You need to stand by until Reda shows up in the Ravensthorpe – you will get irregular and time-restricted agreements from him. More data about this technician can be found on the Daily missions page.

Carbon Ingot/Nickel/Tungsten Ingot

The simplest method to acquire this material is to discover yellow ingot symbols on the guide. They can hole up behind the yellow dabs and represent a chest with an ingot or a rival conveying one (his cadaver should be plundered after he's dead).

Then again, you can secure ingots by finishing chasing difficulties from the chasing hovel in the settlement.

Supplies/Raw materials

Both are utilized to back enhancements in the Viking settlement. The most straightforward approach to get them is to finished attacks on monasteries represented on the world guide by symbols of crossed tomahawks. During the assault, search for the huge cases that Eivor should open with the help of another Viking.

You can likewise discover supplies and crude materials in more modest amounts along with another plunder while openly investigating the game world.

Silver

Silver isn't a creating material, yet the fundamental money in the game, which is utilized for a wide range of buys. Silver can be gotten from multiple points of view:

Along with another plunder.

As an award for finishing journeys and occasions.

Gotten for offering superfluous stuff to dealers.

Gotten when different players utilize your Jomsvikings (sleeping shelter in Ravensthorpe).

Specks on the guide - I don't get their meaning?

From the earliest starting point of the game, the guide of the at present navigated grounds will be set apart with various shading spots. This is what could be compared to the question marks from the past pieces of the arrangement - the sparkling dabs educate about fascinating areas and fortunes to visit/obtain.

Fortunately, you don't need to think about what a specific speck implies. At the point when you approach a speck, it will be supplanted by a symbol of an area a collectible.

The significance of speck tones

The dabs show up in three tones - gold, blue and white. The shading shows what sort of areas or insider facts you are managing. This likewise corresponds with the data from the lower right corner of the guide screen, which educates you about your advancement in considering a given area (model in the image above).

A gold spot may imply that it very well may be one of the accompanying:

Ingot

New weapon or covering (Gear)

Book of information (new capacity)

Load with making materials

Little plunder box - these are more modest brilliant dabs on the world guide, which are excluded to investigate a district at 100%.

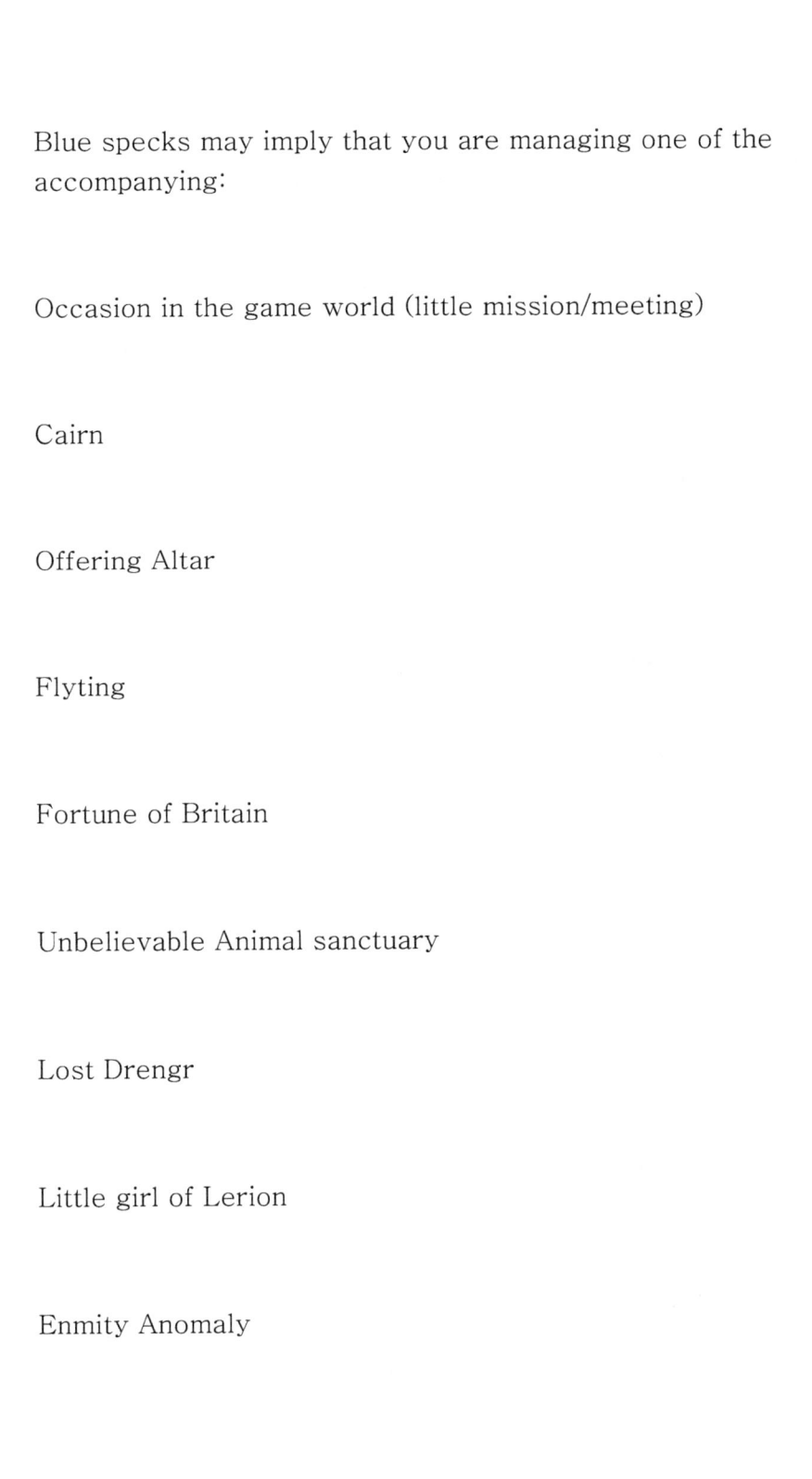

Blue specks may imply that you are managing one of the accompanying:

Occasion in the game world (little mission/meeting)

Cairn

Offering Altar

Flyting

Fortune of Britain

Unbelievable Animal sanctuary

Lost Drengr

Little girl of Lerion

Enmity Anomaly

Standing Stones

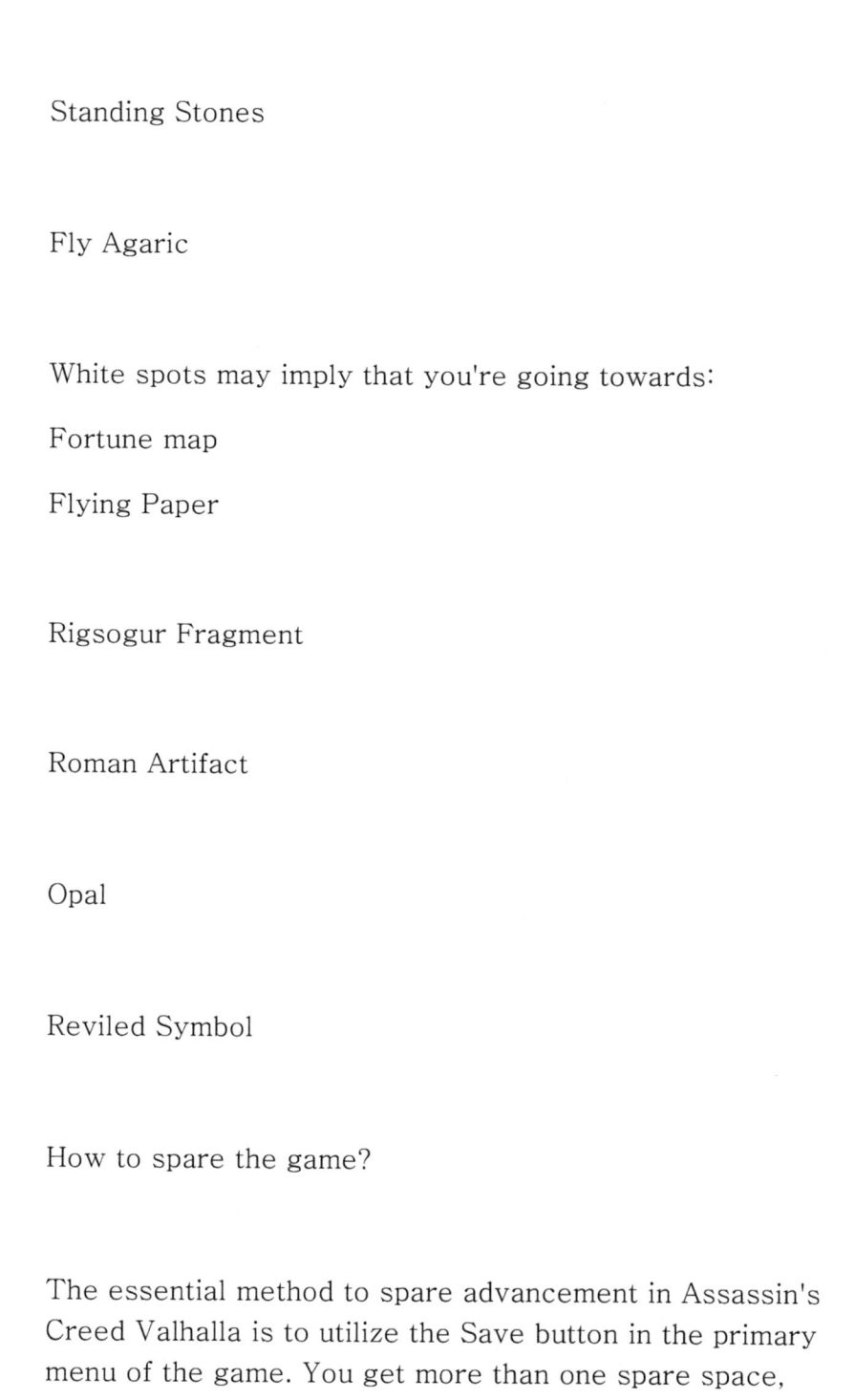

Fly Agaric

White spots may imply that you're going towards:

Fortune map

Flying Paper

Rigsogur Fragment

Roman Artifact

Opal

Reviled Symbol

How to spare the game?

The essential method to spare advancement in Assassin's Creed Valhalla is to utilize the Save button in the primary menu of the game. You get more than one spare space, which empowers you to make a few game states and check, for instance, the results of your decisions. You can likewise utilize the fast spare choice - you can discover it in the extra activity menu. You can open this menu utilizing the accompanying catches:

PC	G
PS4 / PS5	✛
Xbox One / Xbox Series S / Xbox Series X	✚

How does the programmed spare framework work?

Notwithstanding manual sparing, the game guarantees that you don't lose your advancement all alone. The autosave is essentially initiated on significant missions. Additionally, there are a few autosave openings, so it's consistently conceivable to re-visitation of the state prior to settling on a decision in a mission, for instance.

How to change the hour of day?

The fundamental method to change the hour of day in Assassin's Creed Valhalla is to reflect. You can begin the contemplation at most snapshots of the game - a few special cases are being in battle or in length of a significant mission. The reflection choice is accessible in the extra activity menu, which you can open utilizing the catches:

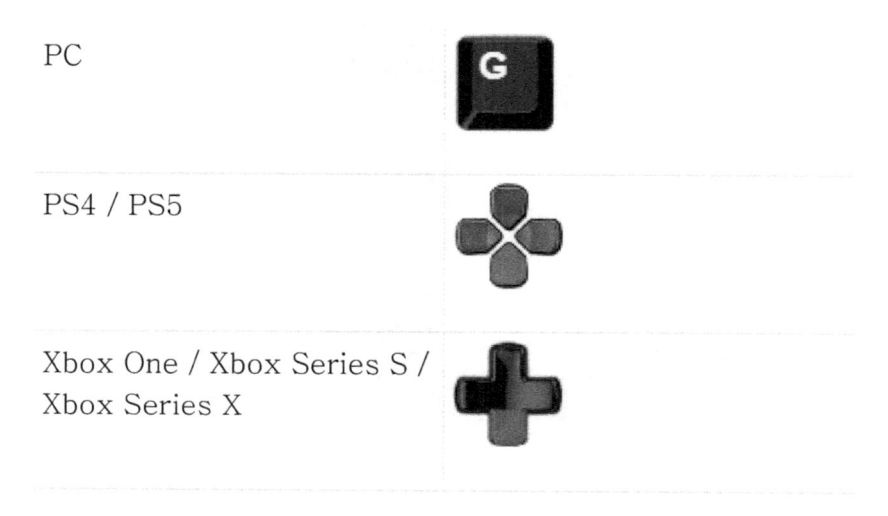

PC	G
PS4 / PS5	
Xbox One / Xbox Series S / Xbox Series X	

It merits adding that you can't pick how long Eivor will reflect. With reflection, you can switch among day and night.

How to open a quick travel choice?

The fundamental purposes of quick travel are those set apart on the guide with the raven symbol. From the start, quick travel to such places is unimaginable, yet in the event that you get to the highest point of such a point it will be forever uncovered - you will have the option to go to the spot whenever ("catching" such focuses likewise empowers you to find significant things and insider facts). You should simply open the guide, select a formerly investigated point, and utilize the quick travel choice.

Quick travel (and guide synchronization) focuses are anything but difficult to perceive – they are high shakes that will be set apart on your compass on the off chance that you are close to them. Make sure to uncover sch focuses each time you see them – they will assist you with investigating the world.

Professional killers Creed Valhalla: Venonis – how to get the gear from the chest?

The mystery is situated in Venonis in the Ledecestrescire area. It is an enormous destroyed structure – you can't get to it from the start on the grounds that the principle entrance is shut and blockaded.

Start by ascending and arriving at the top of the huge structure. Go to its back. In the spot from the image, you can stroll on the line to the overhang on the tree.

Turn right and leap to slide down the rope to the lower gallery.

Presently go to the structure with the mystery. You should utilize a bow and shoot through an opening in the divider – you need to hit the lock on the front entryway.

Wrecking the bar will permit you to utilize the fundamental access to the structure. Manage the rivals or sneak past them.

The chest with the mystery is covered up on the primary floor, behind the sheets appeared in the image – obliterate them. The chest has Hrafn Guard light shield.

Assaults – general data

The assaults are assaults by Vikings on settlements and different areas. Their essential objective is to deny individuals of their most valuable fortunes. The main strike areas are set apart on the guide with a symbol of crossed tomahawks. These are generally nunneries and religious communities situated in England. Be that as it may, you can likewise attack different areas, for example different sorts of campgrounds. The basic component of all strike areas is that they are situated by the water. The strike begins in the wake of arriving at the shore – the Vikings progressively move inland towards the following structures inside the assaulted area.

Significant note – Do not assault areas from locales whose recommended power altogether surpasses Eivor's (for example 160 recommended power when Eivor has 50 force). It will be hard to overcome rivals in these areas. Progress through the game to build Eivor's capacity to coordinate the proposed level of a specific area.

How to begin a strike?

Eivor does each strike along with their Vikings, for example NPCs remaining on your boat. You can begin an assault in two primary manners:

Squeezing the Triangle (PS4/PS5) or Y (Xbox One/Xbox Series X) when moving toward an area that can be struck.

Arriving at the threatening area alone – hold down on the d-cushion and pick the alternative to utilize the horn. It brings your Vikings and the battle will start. The partners will promptly show up close to Eivor – they won't need to begin the fight close to your boat.

Assaults should likewise be possible in an elective manner. Sneak into areas that can be assaulted and utilize the horn after Eivor is identified or when you need the assistance of different Vikings to get remarkable fortunes. On account of this strategy, the attack won't transform into a fight. All things being equal, you can begin it by taking out a portion of the foes with covertness executes.

Strikes - course

During a strike, you will battle with foes in the assaulted area. There is no compelling reason to assault regular citizens - executing a couple of guiltless individuals straight will prompt desynchronization (game over).

Attempt to assault adversaries zeroed in on battling your Vikings. This gives you a superior possibility that they won't have the option to impede or dodge your assaults. It might happen that one of your team individuals will be taken out - the game will stamp this character with a shout mark. You can "restore" that Viking by rushing to them and holding the suitable catch.

Some assaulted areas can likewise have individuals detained in confines. It merits delivering them - quite possibly they will join the battle on your side.

The principle objective of each attack isn't to overcome all adversaries however to ransack the area of the fortunes. These include:

Supplies

Crude Materials

You need supplies and crude materials to fabricate new structures in the Viking settlement. Utilize Odin's Sight to discover them quicker (press the correct simple stick). Symbols of provisions and crude materials are likewise shown on the compass at the highest point of the screen. There are numerous fortunes that need the support of different Vikings – you need them to separate an entryway or move a major front of a holder.

Attacks – different fortunes

The attack closes when all the principle treasures are acquired. Notwithstanding, this doesn't imply that you should leave the area right away. Remain here to discover 100% of its insider facts and plunder. These can be for example objects represented by enormous brilliant spots stamping different Wealth (for example a gold bar or an expertise book) and by little brilliant dabs stamping normal plunder (for example making materials).

Professional killer's Creed Valhalla: Arrows – would i be

able to create them?

How about we start with the data that, naturally, Eivor can convey an exceptionally set number of bolts in the quiver. You can change this by improving the quiver from the stock level. You need to spend making materials for this. The principal redesigns are very modest. For instance, the main quiver overhaul requires just 30 bits of cowhide and 20 iron metals.

Shockingly, Eivor can't deliver bolts on his/her own and subsequently, you need to depend on the bolts found in the game world.

Search essentially for racks and various types of shields, which have a great deal of bolts standing out of them. It is additionally worth inspecting the bodies of vanquished adversaries and untamed life. In the event that the bolt you used to assault an offered foe didn't reprieve, you can get it and use it once more.

On the off chance that you run out of bolts, you can likewise:

Switch bows. There are three sorts of bolts in the game that coordinate three unique kinds of bows – light bow, tracker bow, and hunter bow.

Visit any dealer in the game world (it can likewise be the one from the Viking settlement). They sell each of the three sorts of bolts - they cost from 1 to 3 silver for every piece.

How to crush foes with shields?

Battles with a difficult adversary furnished with a shield can be isolated into a few distinct circumstances:

Go for a covertness assault from behind in the event that you get an opportunity. To do this you will require a shrouded sharp edge, which you will get in one of the underlying primary journeys. On the off chance that you are not seen, you get an opportunity to slaughter your adversary before he begins utilizing the shield. Scout the environmental factors by utilizing the raven before you attempt to kill the objective. This will permit you to decide the places of the excess foes and permit you to make an arrangement for the impending fight. On the off chance that there is tall grass close by, you can utilize it to get despite the foe's good faith unnoticed.

Another great strategy is to utilize a bow. Above all else, center around focusing on the orange focuses on the rival's body (their feeble focuses). Join these two weapons and use them in your strategies.

In the event that you battling an adversary straightforwardly, you can do the accompanying. Hang tight for the adversary with a huge shield to assault, block it, and afterward rapidly counterattack. Along these lines, you should have the option to hit your rival before he ensures himself with the shield once more.

You ought to likewise recollect about avoiding. It causes you to try not to get injured as well as get despite the foe's good faith. Avoidances permit you to rapidly cover a short distance – you get an opportunity to get despite the foe's good faith and assault. Attempt to join repelling assaults with avoids and back assaults.

Professional killer's Creed Valhalla: Choices – would they say they are in the game?

Indeed, there will be various decisions in Assassin's Creed Valhalla and this is because of the way that the game has numerous highlights of a non-straight RPG. They can be isolated into two principle gatherings:

The principal class is the minor decisions. They are portrayed by the way that they don't significantly affect the mission. The chose exchange or conduct alternative may, for instance, influence the course of a solitary discussion or marginally change a piece of a solitary mission. In any case, these are not significant changes.

The subsequent class is major and significant decisions, for example those that can visibly affect the further course of the mission. These decisions can impact, for instance, how the characters will carry on at key snapshots of the plot or whether Eivor will figure out how to pick up significant partners in their triumphs. An illustration of the best option is appeared in the image above - when arranging your first excursion to England you can choose to take the recently obtained supplies or leave them in Norway. Your choice will impact Styrbjorn's demeanor towards the hero.

The game has more than one consummation. The completion will rely upon significant decisions made at key snapshots of the mission.

Shockingly, the game doesn't stamp significant decisions in any capacity. We suggest creating a brisk spare before every discussion so you can do it again and carry on in an alternate manner. You can likewise investigate our walkthrough, in which we included significant choices and their short and long haul results.

Professional killer's Creed Valhalla: Regions/domains - investigation request?

Every district in the game is depicted by the recommended power. This component is depicted in more detail on a different page – Suggested power. So, attempt to go through domains whose recommended power level is near or just marginally higher than Eivor's present one. You can expand your saint's capacity by step up and opening new abilities from the aptitude tree.

On the off chance that you need to begin investigating more troublesome districts quicker, center around exercises that reward you with a lot of XP – principle journeys, occasions on the world guide, and search for greater privileged insights. You can discover more tips on the best way to pick up experience focuses on Gaining XP quicker page.

Here is the recommended request of investigating the areas:

Norway – Rygjafylke – This is a "beginning" area and there is no proposed power. Attempt to investigate it however much as could reasonably be expected prior to going to England.

Try not to investigate Horadfylke in Norway yet. It has an exceptionally high recommended power (280). Re-visitation of this area subsequent to gaining enough ground.

Britain - Mercia - Ledecestrescire - proposed power is 20

Britain - Mercia - Grantebridgescire - proposed power is 20

Britain - Eastern England - proposed power is 55

Britain - Mercia - Oxenefordscire - proposed power is 90

Britain - Mercia - Lunden - recommended power is 90

Britain - Mercia - Sciropescire - recommended power is 130

Britain - Wessex - Cent - recommended power is 130

Britain - Mercia - Lincolnscire - proposed power is 160

Britain - Wessex - Essexe - recommended power is 160

Britain - Wessex - Suthsexe - recommended power is 160

Britain - Northumbria - Eurvicscire - recommended power is 190

Britain - Northumbria - Jorvik - recommended power is 190

Britain - Mercia - Glowecestrescire - proposed power is 220

Britain - Northumbria - Snothighamscire - proposed power is 250

Britain - Wessex - Wincestre - proposed power is 250

Norway - Hordafylke - recommended power is 280

Britain - Wessex - Hamtunscire - recommended power is 340

Professional killers Creed Valhalla: Grind - is it extreme?

On this page of the guide you will discover data whether the granulate in Assassin's Creed Valhalla is long and tiring. We clarify explicitly whether it is important to finish an enormous number of side missions and exercises all together for the saint to have the option to perform story undertakings.

The Grind in AC Valhalla is available somewhat, for example you should know that you might be compelled to procure extra insight/aptitude focuses to have the option to finish story missions. Luckily, pound isn't as genuine as in the past adaptation of the arrangement - Assassin's Creed Odyssey.

Eivor's advancement in the game is controlled by his capacity level, which we have portrayed in more detail on the Suggested Regional Power page. Abstain from investigating districts and finishing journeys set apart in red. These are the markings that educate you that finishing a given movement/mission might be excessively hard for your legend. It is ideal to re-visitation of every single such journey or exercises simply subsequent to making Eivor more grounded, for example raising its capacity level.

There is no requirement for granulating on the off chance that you need to proceed with story missions. The suggested power level for the areas where the following primary missions are incorporated is gradually expanding. More often than not you should do well without finishing side exercises that ensure xp.

The story missions can be finished effectively regardless of whether you have a marginally lower level than suggested, for example 10-15 focuses lower. And, after its all said and done, Eivor should have the option to adapt to the majority of the battles and threatening showdowns that happen inside the errand. The exemption can be troublesome manager fights that are mandatory.

There are no xp supporters in the game, yet the game contains various methods of rapidly assembling experience and expertise focuses. You can, in addition to other things, participate in well compensated occasions in the game world, or visit the side areas, which give extra XP. This ought to permit you to expand the current saint's capacity level to the suggested one in very agreeable conditions.

Themain plot itself is long and will most likely take you a few dozen hours to finish. In any case, this isn't a direct result of the need to granulate for quite a long time prior to beginning the following primary assignment, however essentially due to the huge number of principle missions and storylines needed to finish the game.

Some discretionary exercises might be more troublesome, for example battling troublesome battles with aficionados, Lerion's little girls, or unbelievable creatures. In any case, all such exercises can be deferred and none of them will be lost (aside from time-restricted day by day missions).

Asgard – how to move to it?

Asgard is the land known from Nordic folklore. It is occupied by Nordic divine beings and fills in as the Viking heaven.

Professional killer's Creed Valhalla empowers you to move to Asgard inside one of the storylines. You can go through a few hours in Asgard (in the event that you choose to find everything). There is an entire arrangement of journeys to finish. Moreover, new collectibles and occasions are covered up on new guides. The game will empower you to "move" the things you have procured in Asgard to the principle part of the game.

Moving to Asgard is conceivable with Valka's assistance. After one of your profits to Ravensthorpe, you will be educated that a prophet has showed up in the settlement. Welcome Valka in the harbor and go with her to her quarters.

Tragically, you can't utilize Valka's assistance immediately, on the grounds that first, you need to assemble the Seer's Hut. It is worked close to the cascade at the rear of the primary structure of the settlement. It takes 800 structure materials and 60 crude materials to build it.

As a feature of the following mission, brought In Dreams, you will likewise have to get a thorn for the prophet. At the rear of the cottage you will discover a pitcher of oil. Stroll with it towards the cascade and toss the pitcher at the debilitated divider holed up behind the cascade. This will open admittance to the cavern where thorns develop.

Valka will set up a solution for Eivor, which empowers the hero to nod off and "move" to Asgard. It is important now that the choice isn't irreversible - you will have the option to effortlessly re-visitation of "this present reality" and we depicted it at the lower part of the page.

Asgard - principle attractions

During your stay in Asgard, you will discover a totally new questline, framing a different adventure. When you arrive at Asgard, you can go to the primary mission marker. You don't need to finish the journeys in a steady progression. The game empowers you to re-visitation of Asgard commonly and continue incomplete missions.

You don't need to manage missions in Asgard and you can likewise take a stab at investigating the area. You can discover new insider facts and collectibles, just as partake in new occasions, which, as in the fundamental piece of the game, are compensated with a great deal of XP.

How to leave Asgard?

Asgard can be left openly. The special case is the point at which you're doing some significant piece of the journey. You may then be compelled to finish it before.

In various pieces of Asgard, you can discover intractive entryways.

You can likewise choose a gateway immediately from the world guide - it functions as a quick travel mode.

In the event that you need to go to Asgard once more, have Valka set up another portion of her elixir inside the soothsayer's hovel.

Professional killers Creed Valhalla: Traitor - who sold out Soma?

The subject of the deceiver begins when you do the adventure (arrangement of journeys) in the Grantebridgescire district. Eivor meets with Soma the pioneer and, in addition to other things, encourages her recapture command over the Grantebridge settlement.

Soma's confided in hover of counselors/chiefs incorporates Birna, Galinn and Lif. During this storyline, you will gain from Soma that one of these individuals is a double crosser – has helped out Wigimund and made it simpler for him to vanquish Grantebridge utilizing misdirection.

Eivor is entrusted with researching the backstabber's personality – you can examine the passage underneath the fundamental settlement building, question Grantebridge individuals, and search for a boat. Eivor can likewise meet with every one of Soma's chiefs and complete related minor undertakings.

We have examined this examination in detail in our walkthrough, explicitly in the segment about the primary missions in the Grantebridgescire district.

Finally, you should re-visitation of Soma. You can present to her all the proof you found and data about her counselors, and settle on a choice.

The backstabber is Galinn. The game may mistake you for the way that Lin had yellow paint, yet it was taken and used to assist foes with penetrating the settlement. Galinn will be executed right away.

On the off chance that you recognize some unacceptable deceiver, the two leftover chiefs will at last kick the bucket – one following (being executed by Soma) and the other later by Galinn. You will likewise have an extra manager battle with Galinn. Some unacceptable decision will obviously deteriorate your connection with Soma fundamentally.

Professional killers Creed Valhalla: Traitor – who sold out Rollo?

You will find out about the backstabber during the Old Wounds fundamental journey, where Eivor needs to meet Rollo in a camp in the Essexe district.

The two individuals suspects, Gerhildand Lork, are being held in Rollo's camp.

You can ask them inquiries, just as check out the camp for extra pieces of information – they will be set apart with blue mists when utilizing Odin's Sight. A few follows can open new exchange choices – ask the two detainees inquiries again to check what new you can realize.

Gerhild is the trickster – converse with Rollo and show him the gathered proof.

In the event that you settle on some unacceptable decision, for example in the event that you pick Lork as a swindler, Estrid will get injured sooner rather than later (she will get harmed yet she won't pass on). Nonetheless, the choice about the deceiver won't influence Rollo's disposition towards Eivor – you will consistently have the option to depend on his assistance all through the remainder of the game (he will join the Viking settlement as a Jomsviking subsequent to finishing the Essexe storyline).

How to get to Vinland?

Vinland is a totally isolated land, which you can't at first visit. You won't discover it in the map book used to choose the terrains.

To open admittance to Vinland you just need to arrive at a specific point in the plot. In particular, you need to finish the Lunden storyline, the one where you help Stowe and Erke and kill a few individuals from the Ancient Order. At the point when you re-visitation of Randvi in Ravensthorpe, you will open In a Strange Land mission and discover that Hytham from the Hidden Office might want to converse with you. In your discussion with Hytham, you will find that Gorm, child of Kjotve the Cruel and one of the Ancient Order's Masters, has recently disappeared to Vinland.

Re-visitation of Randvi. Vinland will show up on the Alliance Map – you will discover it at the exceptionally base. You can choose it as another adventure/mission line.

It is significant now that Vinland doesn't have the suggested locale power, for example you can visit it at any phase of the game. Stand by with going to Vinland until you've updated proportions by a couple of levels, to have a greater amount of them when you arrive at the area.

To go to Vinland, you should meet Nessa at the docks of Ravensthorpe and affirm your will to go on half a month's excursion.

An outing to Vinland isn't an excursion without a fast return. Regardless of whether you need to re-visitation of England rashly in the wake of arriving at Vinland, the game will permit you to do as such. All resulting goes among England and Vinland will be free.

Vinland – what's going on here?

The name Vinland sounds exceptionally baffling, yet it is truly about the North America from the hour of the Viking successes.

Eivor, upon appearance in Vinland, will meet cordial Iroquois. Regardless of the language hindrance, the Indians will offer help as hardware to get by in an obscure climate.

Despite the fact that Vinland/North America is a tremendous mainland, the place where there is Vinland in the game isn't broad. Eivor is given a little region to investigate, which, best case scenario, will keep going for a couple of long periods of cautious investigation.

Vinland - undertaking subtleties

Eivor can't take with him the gear used to investigate the fundamental game terrains, to be specific England and Norway. This is disclosed by the need to take on the appearance of a slave (Thrall) to make it simpler to get Gorm, who is the principle focus of the campaign to Vinland. Eivor's gear will obviously be sitting tight for him when he re-visitations of England. You won't lose it.

You will begin your visit to Vinland with a practically vacant stock. You need to manage without:

Primary weapons and conceivable shield

Shield components

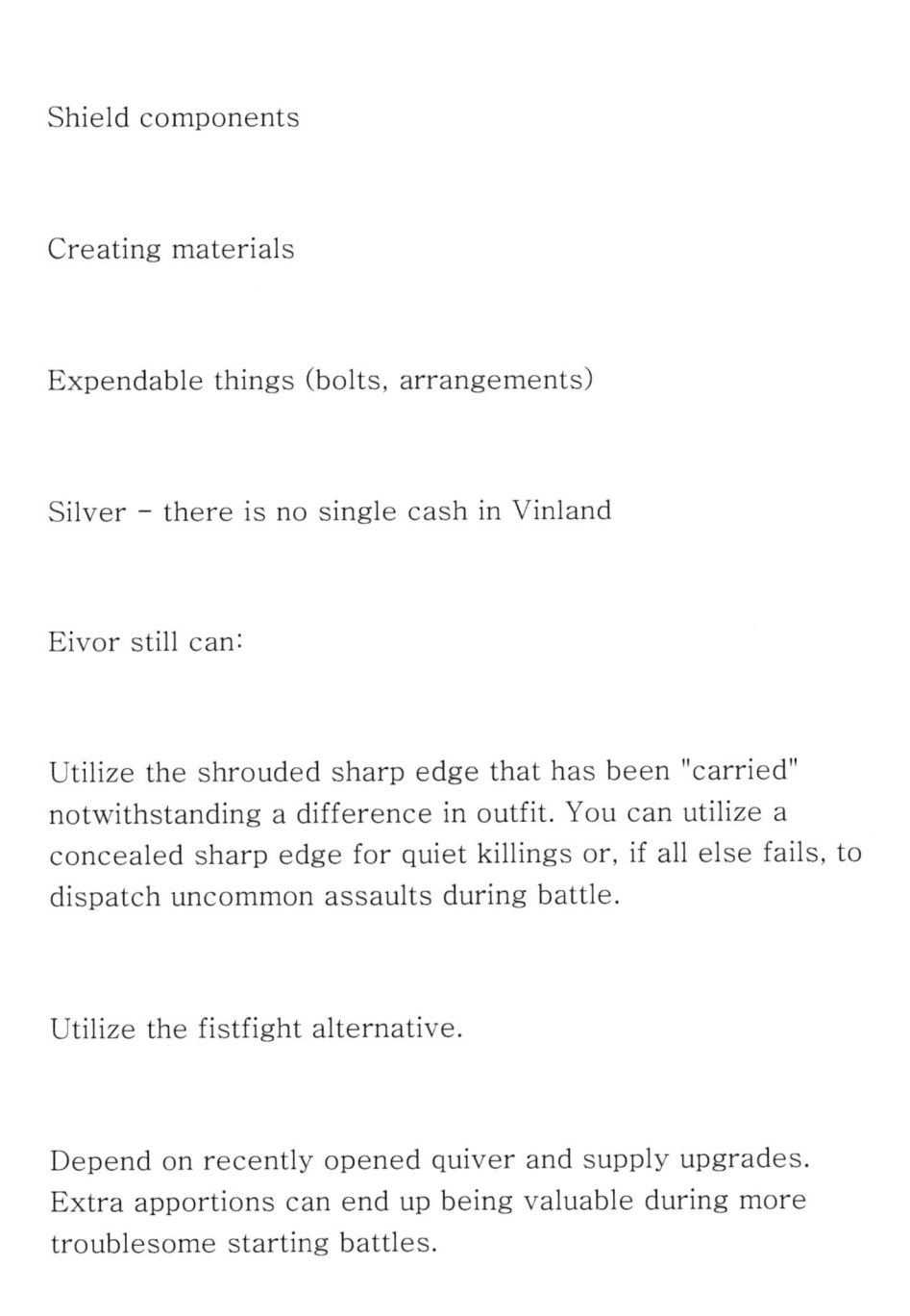

Creating materials

Expendable things (bolts, arrangements)

Silver - there is no single cash in Vinland

Eivor still can:

Utilize the shrouded sharp edge that has been "carried" notwithstanding a difference in outfit. You can utilize a concealed sharp edge for quiet killings or, if all else fails, to dispatch uncommon assaults during battle.

Utilize the fistfight alternative.

Depend on recently opened quiver and supply upgrades. Extra apportions can end up being valuable during more troublesome starting battles.

In Vinland you can get new gear. The game doesn't drive this progression, however the more new hardware you get, the simpler it will be to manage furnished adversaries from adversary camps and Gorm himself.

New things of gear should be bought from sellers. You will discover a few of them on the guide – they all offer very similar things. Need buys are skirmish weapons (there are two distinct ones to browse) and a bow, so you can begin adequately assaulting foes and wild creatures right up front and distance battles.

Things showed by traders must be paid for with making materials Common materials can be found in little cartons and in the cadavers of murdered creatures.

Ingots are more hazardous. Chests with ingots can be found in unfriendly camps. They are constantly bolted and you should initially execute the adversary who has the way in to the chest. Fortunately you will discover 2 ingots in each crate.

In the event that you need, you can attempt to get an Arenhare'ko:wa protective layer set notwithstanding a skirmish weapon and bow – it is appeared in the connected picture. This will permit to get two rewards to measurements:

Accomplish more distance harm if Eivor is in full wellbeing.

Wellbeing recuperation if your wellbeing has dipped under half.

Tragically, the Indian defensive layer can't be utilized in England. It is just accessible for the length of your stay in the place where there is Vinland and can supplant the default slave attire.

In Vinland you can discover vantage focuses, threatening camps, loot, and secrets. Vinland's just resources are the chests with ingots. If there should be an occurrence of privileged insights, these include interesting occasions just as discretionary exercises (for example new hill or new battle with unbelievable creature). You can do all the discretionary stuff consistently or simply after you've finished the primary story in Vinland. The game won't surge you to leave this land.

Interestingly, after Eivor's demise you won't see the game over screen, yet you will be moved to the principle Iroquois camp. You will discover that you have been relieved and you can continue the game.

How to re-visitation of England?

Leaving Vinland is conceivable whenever of the game, even after appearance in this land. You need to converse with Nessa or Hilde on the shore and affirm your desire to re-visitation of England.

On the off chance that you need to visit Vinland again later in the game, it is most effortless to do it by calling the map book in the guide menu (press Triangle/Y). You can pick Vinland from the rundown of known terrains.

Is there grown-up substance in the game?

In Assassin's Creed Valhalla , grown-up substance is showing up all through lion's share of the game. Most importantly, this included wicked and vicious battle, yet in addition sexual topics, liquor, psychedelic drugs or swearing. Executions or other terrific methods of murdering adversaries are regularly portrayed. There are additionally scenes with topless ladies or components of sentiment with different characters. The game additionally offers drinking rivalries or missions identified with the utilization of different medications.

How to restrict content unsatisfactory for minors?

The game offers the chance of restricting substance unsatisfactory for minors – albeit just somewhat. In the game alternatives (in the tab committed to interactivity) there is a segment with delicate substance. There you can kill the areas of merciless executions in battle and dissection, limit the measure of blood and conceal nakedness.

Professional killers Creed Valhalla: Yellow longship – where to discover it?

Throughout the Stench of Treachery mission, you should lead an examination to uncover Soma's double crosser. Just three of her believed individuals were among the suspects: Galinn, Lif and Birna.

One of the critical tips to assist you with finding the fact of the matter is the yellow longship surrendered some place in the swamps. For simplicity of reference, we have denoted its area in the image above.

Make sure to painstakingly inspect the relinquished boat and read the short note that is inside the vessel.

Professional killers Creed Valhalla: Dag's hatchet – offer it to him or not?

As an update, Dag is one of the more noticeable Vikings in the settlement. From the earliest starting point, he will show that he doesn't care for Eivor. At the point when Sigurd leaves the settlement incidentally, Dag will continue sabotaging Eivor's choices just as the choice of giving over control over the group to Eivor during the jarl's nonattendance.

The contention with Dag will develop much greater subsequent to finishing the storyline of the Cent area, for example in the wake of setting up that Fulke is tormenting the hijacked Sigurd. After you finish the Cent adventure and "close it" at the Alliance table, another journey called A Brewing Storm will show up in your diary. Follow its portrayal and rest in Eivora's room in the principle working of Ravensthorpe.

Dag's yells will awaken Eivor – he is holding up external the structure. Dag will challenge Eivor to a duel for assuming control over the initiative of the faction.

Shockingly, you can't reject Dag. Regardless of whether you reject his test, you will even now at last stand up to him. The decision of the exchange alternative hence doesn't make a difference.

You should overcome Dag and this showdown is treated as a supervisor battle.

The subsequent option, and considerably more significant, anticipates you just in the wake of winning the battle – when Eivor will remain over the withering Dag. You can:

Hand over the hatchet to Dag and let him enter Valhalla in the afterlife.

Decline to hand over the hatchet to Dag and lead to his outcast to Helheim.

The choice about Dag's hatchet influences Sigurd's demeanor towards Eivor. After Sigurd is spared and gotten back to Ravensthorpe, he will visit Dag's grave.

On the off chance that you gave the hatchet to Dag, Sigurd will be satisfied. This is one of the decisions that may carry Sigurd closer to remaining in Anglia toward the finish of the game.

On the off chance that you denied giving Dag his hatchet, Sigurd will be irate. This is one of the decisions that may carry Sigurd closer to getting back to Norway toward the finish of the game.

Sentiments - essentials

Professional killer's Creed Valhalla allows you to sentiment with chose characters. This works correspondingly to AC Odyssey – in the wake of meeting a potential sentiment competitor you can find a way to enter a closer relationship with them. From that point onward, you will have the option to kiss/lay down with them/enter a relationship.

There are less "huge" sentiments in AC Valhalla than in Odyssey, however they are a smidgen more broad. These are not, at this point simply short scenes in which you just pick the discourse choice set apart with a heart. Eivor may need to make more strides prior to having an unsanctioned romance with somebody. Rather than going through just a single night with an individual, it is conceivable to go into a more genuine connection with them.

Sentiment choices are accessible paying little heed to Eivor's sex, for example you can sentiment every one of the characters recorded in this section whether or not you are playing as a lady or a man. On the off chance that you need to perceive how a given sentiment looks like for the two sexes, spare the game prior to beginning it. This will permit you to re-visitation of the past point, change your sex, and start a closer relationship with a similar NPC once more.

Aside from the principle sentiments, there are still choices to go through short close minutes with chosen NPCs. This classification incorporates, among others, a lady named Bil. In one of the occasions in Norway, you can help her discover a brush.

Professional killers Creed Valhalla: Petra - sentiment

Petra is a tracker. You can meet her unexpectedly by building a tracker's cabin in the settlement - this structure is accessible after the settlement arrives at level two. To construct a tracker's cottage, you need 600 structure materials and 45 crude materials.

During your first discussion with Petra, you will find out about her calling and that she runs a "chasing business" along with her sibling Wallace, who is a leather treater. You can bring Wallace prizes of standard and incredible creatures, however this isn't identified with the alternative of having a sentiment with Petra.

During one of the following visits to the settlement, Petra may approach Eivor for help. You will get some answers concerning her sibling's vanishing. You can go with the lady - this will begin Have You Seen This Man? side journey.

The full portrayal of that journey can be found in the

walkthrough area. It includes, in addition to other things, exploring where Wallace was seen once and for all, experiencing a white elk, battling wolves, and encountering different mental trips.

At the point when you re-visitation of the settlement, discover Petra and converse with her. Pick the exchange choice set apart with a heart - you can go on a "date" to the shooting range.

During the shooting rivalry the principal individual to score 10, 15 or 25 focuses will win. You can win or leave Peter alone the first - it doesn't make a difference.

After the date you can meet Petra once more. She will uncover her affections for Eivor and propose a more genuine relationship. You can pick the choice to show your sentiments - you will kiss Petra.

The activity will move to Eivor's room in the primary structure of the settlement. Eivor will lay down with Petra (no simulated intercourses in the game, the screen will be obscured and the game will show the structure from outside).

After some time, a discussion symbol will show up over

Petra's head. During this and all ensuing gatherings with Petra you can:

Go out on the town with Petra – you can contend at the shooting range, have an intoxicated rivalry or play dice (orlog).

Kiss Petra.

Lay down with Petra.

Part ways with Petra – this isn't needed to begin another sentiment, you can essentially disregard this choice.

Professional killers Creed Valhalla: Broder sentiment

Broder is a Danish champion experienced when you play through the story line in the East Anglia locale, the one about assisting Oswald with being picked as the ruler of this land.

The principal showdown with Brother and his partner Brither will occur during the dinner (fundamental journey Kingmaker). The battle will begin and you should beat the

Danes in a fistfight. Luckily, this battle won't prompt anybody's demise. It will likewise not influence your odds to sentiment Broder.

For an extremely significant time-frame nothing will happen with regards to building up nearer relations with the Dane. You should finish subsequen principle journeys in New Anglia until you arrive at the last assignment of this territory - Wedding Horns, identified with Oswald's wedding.

Eivor can experience different characters welcome to the wedding and take part in discretionary exercises with them. You can likewise meet Oswald himself and go along with him in a drinking rivalry, which is a little cadenced game. It doesn't make a difference whether you win or lose the opposition, or whether you choose to wager your own silver.

Approach the table with nourishment for the wedding visitors. This will start another discussion with Broder.

During the new discussion, Broder will begin playing forcefully with Eivor. Pick a discourse choice set apart with the heart symbol to react to his advances.

After another trade of perspectives, affirm that you need to go with Broder to a more segregated spot.

You can watch a kissing scene with Broder. After it is finished, you will re-visitation of the wedding grounds.

Just to remind, the man you kissed with is Broder - select the second exchange alternative from the rundown.

You can meet Broder by and by in the last piece of the assignment, explicitly when leaving New Anglia. Broder remains before the primary structure of the settlement and you can bid farewell to him.

Professional killers Creed Valhalla: Randvi - sentiment

Randvi is the spouse of Siegfried, Eivor's cultivate sibling. She shows up from the earliest starting point of the game since she lives in Fornburg town in Norway. Randvi joins the Vikings, who will vanquish England. Starting now and into the foreseeable future you can meet her in the principle working of the settlement. Randvi remains at the table with the Alliance Map, and you need to meet all her occasions you plan campaigns to new terrains to obtain more partners.

From discussions with Randvi, you will discover that her union with Siegfried was organized the purpose of two distinct Vikings tribes and that she doesn't have profound affections for her significant other. It didn't assist Randvi's relationship with Siegfried that before the occasions introduced in the game, Siegfried invested a ton of energy in victories, while Randvi lived alone in Fornburg.

A side mission Taken for Granted is related with Randvi. The occasion to begin this mission comes when you ask Randvi how she's doing. This "brilliant" discourse alternative ought to show up during the gathering with Randvi after three unions have been framed and in the wake of finishing the journey line in the Grantebridgescire locale. As an update, this is a progression of journeys identified with Soma and choosing the backstabber in her positions.

Randvi is audacious, and her journey is to invest free energy with her. The main assignment in this journey is to arrive at the Grantebridge settlement. Randvi will ask not to utilize the boat. You can swim over the stream with her or utilize your pony in the event that it has passed swimming preparing.

In the wake of arriving at Grantebridge, the characters will have the option to meet with Magnim and help the individuals of Grantebridge to dispose of new outlaws. It is ideal to offer your assistance, particularly as overcoming the outlaws won't be exceptionally troublesome (it is ideal to debilitate the goliath with an unexpected assault or spare it for the end).

In the wake of accepting thanks from Magni, Randvi will offer to partake in the drinking rivalry. It is best not to decay since whether winning or losing (it is a small musical game) won't influence your odds to sentiment her.

Somewhere else that Eivor and Randvi choose to visit is the remains of the Sunken Tower. At the point when you arrive, you need to begin climbing the pinnacle. Try not to attempt to arrive at the top (perspective). You simply need to arrive at the little rack beneath.

From that point forward, a cutscene during which Randvi will precipitously kiss Eivor will play,

You can pick a discourse choice set apart with a heart so Eivor will affirm that he responds the inclination.

You will see a cutscene incorporating laying down with Randvi. The following day, Eivor will awaken without Randvi next to him and will discover that Randvi has gotten back to the Ravensthorpe.

You can at present meet with Randvi. To do this you need to re-visitation of the fundamental structure in the settlement and converse with her. You can:

Kiss Randvi.

Lay down with Randvi.

Say a final farewell to Randvi – this isn't needed to begin another sentiment, you can just overlook this choice.

Professional killers Creed Valhalla: Estrid – sentiment

Estrid is the spouse of Birstan, the leader of Essexe. The principal meeting with Estrid will happen soon after the start of the adventure (storyline) of the Essexe area. The lady at first remains in Colcestre town.

From the primary gatherings and the codex section about Estrid, you will discover that she lives in a troubled organized marriage she had to do when she was as yet a youthful aristocrat. Birstan thinks more about campaigns than his own significant other. During the journeys occurring in Essexe, you will for example seize Estrid with her consent to help her leave Anglia and re-visitation of her country.

The opportunity to lay down with Estrid comes after the phony grabbing – during the Taken fundamental mission. The discussion with Estrid will occur in a temporary camp. The lady will welcome Eivor to talk in private. You need to consent to it before you leave the camp and set off to meet with Birstan during the Twists and Turns fundamental mission.

You will discover Estrid sitting on a cover in the camp, close to a major tree.

From the discussion with Estrid, you will discover that she prefers Eivor and that she might want to hang out. You can pick an exchange alternative set apart with a heart with a bolt to state that you feel the equivalent.

Eivor will lay down with Estrid. Sadly, this is just a passing issue and once the game is continued, you should proceed with the Essexe area's storyline.

Professional killers Creed Valhalla: Tewdwr - sentiment

Tewdwr is a future cleric, who is one of the contender to turn into the head of Glowecestre. The principal meeting with Tewdwer happens consequently while doing the storyline of the Glowecestrescire locale. Tewdwr is one of the companions of the metal forger Gunnar, who came to Glowecestre to propose to Brigid.

(What could be compared to present day Halloween), you will have the option to get tanked along with Tewdwr.

During the discussion, you can pick the discourse alternative set apart with a heart and reveal to Tewdwr that you like him. Nothing will emerge from this yet.

The opportunity to sentiment Tewdwer shows up simply subsequent to finishing the adventure in the Glowecestrescire locale, for example in the wake of finishing The Burning of the Wicker Man fundamental mission. You will get a letter from Tewdwer welcoming you to visit him (check the letterbox in the principle working of the settlement).

Re-visitation of Glowecestre, explicitly to where the straw structure was scorched. Subsequent to conversing with Tewdwr, you can again choose the exchange with the heart symbol to begin being a tease.

Pick another exchange alternative, this time affirming that you need Tewdwr.

You will a cut-scene during which your character and Tewdwr will kiss. From that point onward, Eivor will bid farewell to the man.

Professional killers Creed Valhalla: Vili - sentiment

Vili is somebody who Eivor knows well indeed - they have been companions since adolescence. Vili is the child of jarl Hemmingson who runs the Snotinghamscire locale. You will meet Vili while doing the principle missions related with the Snotinghamscire storyline. During one of them, Eivor should help the perishing jarl pick his replacement.

You should invest very some energy with the game to have the option to begin romancing Vili. This will occur at the finish of the Snotinghamscire adventure, during the Under the Skin journey which happens after the passing of a jarl and the underlying choice of his replacement.

In the wake of experiencing the mine with Vili, you will get have the option to converse with him in the camp. During the discussion, Vili will start to review the past and the lost possibility of a closer relationship. You can say that you are additionally contemplating what may have occurred.

Select the exchange choice affirming that you need Vili.

Eivor and Vili will begin kissing and lay down with one another. The following morning, the characters will concur that this was just a brief undertaking, yet they will stay dear companions.

It is significant that if toward the finish of the Snotinghamscire storyline you picked Trygve for the following yarl, Vili will have the option to move to Ravensthorpe and join the Raven Clan as one of the Jomsvikings. You will have the option to make him a player in the Drakkar's team.

The Seas of Fate

The determination happens in the last phase of the Sea of Destination mission. Before the undertaking to England, Sigurd asks Eivor how to deal with the provisions. Taking the provisions to England won't be good for Sigurd, particularly since they recently had a place with Kjotve. On the off chance that you choose to leave the provisions to Styrbjorn in Fornburg, you will get Sigurd's endorsement, which will impact his last evaluation of Eivor as a pioneer.

Mourned – execute or spare?

Regretted kicks the bucket: Eivor executes Rued promptly (his body can't be plundered). Oswald won't support of this choice and will give a discourse about the way that murdering prompts nothing. Individuals need to change to keep up harmony in East Anglia. Notwithstanding everything, he will at present be Eivor's partner. Killing the foe additionally forestalls Oswald's wedding with Valdis being hindered – you would need to battle Rued for the subsequent time. Furthermore, Finnr will join Eivor's group.

Lamented lives: Oswald will be satisfied with your choice and will give a discourse about the leniency that suits each fighter, even the fiercest ones. In the event that you let Rued live, he will show up later at Oswald's and Valdis' wedding, where he will assault the King of East Anglia.

Who should battle Rued – Oswald or Eivor?

Eivor battles for the ruler: Rued is murdered by Eivor and the recently delegated lord Oswald will be satisfied with this. He will swear devotion to the Raven Clan. In addition, Finnr will join Eivor's team;

Oswald battles: Oswald will battle and win, in this manner picking up the regard and enthusiasm for all the visitors. He won't slaughter Rued. All things considered, he banishes the man from his realm. Finnr will be so dazzled by the new ruler's accomplishment that he will remain close by and won't join Eivor.

The Billhook

Piece of information 1/2 – Kill an individual from the Order called The Vellum. This is one of individuals depicted on the page about Maegester 4 – The Vice. Then again, you can execute an individual from the Order called The Anvil – we portrayed him in the following subsection.

Piece of information 2/2 – Visit Aelfgarstun situated in the western piece of the Lincolnscire area. The hint is in one of the cabins.

Havelok – The Billhook is situated in the northern piece of the city of Lincoln in the Lincolnscire area. You can discover him before one of the cottages or inside the structure.

The Anvil

Hint 1/2 – Kill an individual from the Order called The Scabbard.

Piece of information 2/2 – Visit Saint Albanes Abbey situated in the Oxenefordscire locale. You can discover the piece of information in the manufacture. In the event that you would prefer not to battle, sneak into the produce to evade foes in the nunnery. You don't have to begin a strike.

Patrick – The Anvil is situated in Oxenforda situated at the western finish of the Oxenefordscire district. You will discover the objective in the manufacture. The most effortless approach to murder Patrick is to utilize the concealed edge. There should be no watchmen in the zone, yet certainly, leave the town rapidly after the death.

The Lathe

Piece of information 1/3 – Kill an extremist named Horsa. He goes on the fringe of the Oxenefordscire and Grantebridgescire districts (look at the page committed to the extremists).

Piece of information 2/3 – Visit Buckingham in the Oxenefordscire area. You need to crush the nearby orlog player (a dice smaller than normal game).

Piece of information 3/3 – Go to Eatun Barn neighboring Oxeneforda at the western finish of the Oxenefordscire area. The hint is in the cavern, which is gotten to by a debilitated divider – utilize a dangerous shot or toss a red container with oil at the divider.

Mucel – The Lathe is in Buckingham in Oxenefordscire. The objective can be discovered strolling around the town and it is ideal to assault him in some detached spot (or possibly away from the gatekeepers).

The Ash-Spear

Piece of information 1/2 – Kill an extremist named Wuffa. He goes in the East Anglia locale (go to the page about the devotees).

Piece of information 2/2 – Go to the Ruined Tower, one of the quick travel focuses in the East Anglia district. The piece of information can be found on the truck at the base of the pinnacle.

Gifle – The Ash-Spear remains in a den in the Forest Hideout, situated in the East Anglia locale, east of Grantebridge town. You don't need to slaughter all adversaries from the camp. You should simply to slaughter the Gifle himself – you can crush him in an open encounter or utilizing covertness (ideally with a fortified concealed edge, since this is a first class adversary).

The Tang

Wigmund – The Tang is an individual from the Order. You

will overcome him during the mission, explicitly the storyline related with the Grantebridgescire locale. The paladin is stowing away in the Isle of Ely Monastery visited as a component of the fundamental journey An Island of Eels. You can assault the monastery or sneak into it and murder Wigmund with an unexpected assault.

The Crozier

Diocesan Herferith – The Crozier is an individual from the Order. You will overcome him during the mission, explicitly the storyline related with the Lincolnscire district. The snapshot of finding that the diocesan is an individual from the Order relies upon how you vote during the Lincolnscire adventure. You can't skirt the second when you need to kill him.

Maegester – The Lyre

Tatfrid is Maegester The Lyre. His character is found naturally in the wake of distinguishing and murdering 6 different individuals from the Orde.

Tatfrid is situated in Grantebridge in the Grantebridgescire locale. He can perform different exercises and stroll around the settlement. As usual, attempt to kill him when there is no one around.

Professional killers Creed Valhalla: Maegester 3 - The Instrument | Order of the Ancients

This is an abnormal Maegester. She is the one in particular who doesn't expect you to dispense with different individuals from the Order of the Ancients. To distinguish the Instrument Maegester - you need to begin a progression of journeys in the Oxenefordscire locale.

The character of the deceiver will be uncovered at the finish of the Oxenefordscire journey line, at the hour of the catch of Siegfried. You will discover that the Maegester is Fulke, the paladin that was delivered in one of the past primary missions.

The game won't permit you to execute Fulke right away. You simply need to proceed with the primary mission. Fulke can be managed while finishing a progression of journeys in the Suthsexe locale. You will face her in the primary mission - Storming the Walls. You need to take on a two-section conflict with Fulke - first in a faintly lit grave and afterward on a superficial level. This fight is depicted in more detail in the Bosseschapter and in our walkthrough.

The Vellum

Sign 1/2 – Kill the individual from the Order known as The Baldric. This is one of individuals portrayed on the page about Maegester 5 – The Keel.

Hint 2/2 – Visit the enormous Thieves' Warren camp situated in the Glowecestrescire locale, north of Glowecestre. The sign is situated inside a blockaded structure, which you can get to from the opening in the floor.

Eanbhert – The Vellum is in the city of Glowecestre. You can discover him in one of the structures in the docks, by the water. Get inside the structure through the opening set apart in the image number 2. You can execute Eanbhert without the danger of cautioning the territory.

The Dart

Hint 1/2 – Kill an individual from the Order known as The Vellum. We portrayed this individual in the past area.

Piece of information 2/2 – Use brisk travel to move to the pinnacle ruins in the Sciropescire district, set apart in picture number 1. Try not to hop off the top of the pinnacle, simply begin moving down gradually. In transit you will pass the open shade from picture 2. It will empower you to get into the live with the hint.

Goodbye, Defender of Otta's Wyrd – The Dart is in Quatford town in the Sciropescire area . At the point when you arrive, visit the corrals where the individual you are searching for works. You can without much of a stretch execute Tata with the shrouded edge.

The Scotchpiper

Sign 1/3 – Kill the extremist known as Cola. He goes close to the outskirts of upwards of four areas – Lincolnscire, Eurviscire, Snotinghamscire and Ledecestrescire (go to the page about extremists).

Hint 2/3 – Visit the town of Ledecestre in the Ledecestrescire district. Discover the symbol of horns – you need to win a drinking little game, which comprises of musical squeezing of a catch and swinging the handle left or right when important. In the event that you fear losing silver, pick the most reduced wager (100 silver) or spare your advancement prior to beginning the smaller than expected game.

Piece of information 3/3 – Visit the town of Cweornic situated in the western piece of the Ledecestrescire locale. The searched after piece of information is inside the most firmly monitored expanding on the slope.

Gunilla – The Scotchpiper is remaining in the town of Repton in Ledecestrescire locale. You can discover the lady dealing with the docks. It is anything but difficult to murder her by bouncing on her from the upper rack and utilizing the shrouded sharp edge.

The Firebrand

Abbess Ingeborg – The Firebrand is an individual from the Order, which you will crush during the mission, explicitly while finishing story line related with the city of Jorvik . Eivor will figure out how to distinguish and dispense with The Firebrand as a component of the fundamental mission called Burning the Firebrand.

Just after Ingeborg is uncovered, she can be executed. Inside the structure there are three ladies and The Firebrand is the person who doesn't have a yellow imprint and a question mark in the name. In the event that you have the ability called Advanced Assassination, you can drop on Ingeborg and slaughter her immediately. Else, you will confront an immediate battle with Ingeborg and her subordinates.

The Needle

Grigorii – The Needle is an individual from the Order that you will overcome while finishing the mission, specifically while experiencing the storyline related with the city of Jorvik . Eivor figures out how to distinguish and wipe out the Needle in the primary mission called Pricking the Needle.

You will have the option to get The Needle in the wake of escaping the sewers. Grigorii is at the commercial center and it is ideal to assault him from one of the rooftops – utilize a bow or drop down on him to utilize the shrouded cutting edge. Anticipate a battle with his protectors and different watchmen from the region.

The Vault

Audun – The Vault is an individual from the Order, whom you will vanquish during the fundamental mission, to be specific while finishing the storyline related with the city of Jorvik. Eivor will have the option to recognize and kill The Vault in the primary journey called Closing the Vault.

The encounter with Audun will occur whether or not or not you accurately select him from individuals present at the gathering. Subsequent to harming the visitors, the man will attempt to get away. Disregard the battles in the theater and follow him. You can slaughter him with a bow or hop him and utilize the sharp edge.

Try not to execute The Vault on the off chance that you experience him at the theater while investigating Jorvik. His sudden passing may harm your spare game information. Audun should just be slaughtered in the wake of finishing the connected mission.

Maegester - The Vice

Maegester - The Vice is Reeve Derby. His character is naturally found after you distinguish and kill the other 6 individuals from the Order portrayed previously.

Reeve Derby is remaining in Picheringa town in Eurvicscire locale. It is ideal to arrive at this area around evening time. There is then a decent possibility that the reeve will rest in his own home. You can slaughter him in his rest.

II. Professional killer's Creed Valhalla tips you need to know prior to lifting your hatchet

1. Use Synin and Odin's Sight

Perhaps it will appear to be a given for Assassin's Creed players yet it's an ideal occasion to use your abilities again. In case you go for the default 'Explorer' setting concerning venture course, you may twist up arbitrarily wandering looking for your next clue. Send up your raven to research things, use the middle limit, and a blue line should manage the bearing toward your goal district. You'll by then observe the zone set apart out in clear blue.

Your other supportive limit, Odin's Sight, comes in helpful to find passing targets yet what's more during attacks. Keep affecting your remarkable vision and you'll identify the staggering gold gleam of product to plunder. They'll by then appear as barrels in your compass at the most noteworthy purpose of the screen. Various fortunes will similarly shimmer splendid gold when you're researching so reliably guarantee you keep an eye, especially concerning pursuing down the limit giving Books of Knowledge.

2. Snatch those sync centers

This one is another given for the Assassin's Creed society yet it justifies rehashing that on account of the meandering aimlessly thought of Valhalla, you need to guarantee you are scaling the nearest hawk symbolled sync centers to get those snappy travel territories. The mission intentionally takes you across nearly the whole guide and you would lean toward not to be the Viking gotten out when you fail to coordinate in a town that you by then need to re-visitation of for an arrangement for Reda, or as an element of the story. Synchronization concentrates furthermore name up towns and regions of premium on your guide so that ends up being valuable during the mission also.

3. Update your distributes early

The switch back to a maintainable prosperity mixture system was an extreme move from Ubisoft and infers that fights can not, now essentially be won by deserting endlessly and returning for even more whenever you're readied. Or maybe you need to make distributes with picked berries and mushrooms that, luckily, are overflowing on the planet. You can even pick them while you're on your mount so ride through food is totally possible. Food will as a rule be extensively open across Mercia in unrefined and cooked structure through fireside pots yet on the off chance that you're concerned, you can similarly buy full allots from close by dealers. You'll start with space for only one pack of distributes yet you can refresh your pockets with resources. Do this early and you'll wind up in less predicaments.

4. Watch your mushrooms

Furthermore, remembering that we're on the subject. Much equivalent to, in light of everything, keep an eye out for your mushroom utilization. While most pickable food is valuable for you, there are different mushroom fixes that will take your prosperity. As a reliable rule, the yellow mushrooms are totally fine yet in case you see some dull fungo, which you'll habitually spot in chided places, remain away if you would incline toward not to watch your prosperity bar fall. Luckily Ubi doesn't appear, apparently, to be mean so anything you find filling in the zone of administrator battles and strikes will be shielded to eat.

5. Pound glass

Everything is fundamentally more, all things considered, smashable this time around. If something looks weak and sensitive, it probably is and that fuses the awesome recolored glass of order and church windows. While some of them are invigorated with metal to thwart segment, there are regularly windows you can pound like a Viking punk with a jolt or ax to move inside. Likewise, in case you can't get in a window, chances are that you can find one to use to shoot the lock on restricted doors. Use Odin's Sight and this square state of wood will highlight in red. This is moreover the circumstance with enticing catch for profound packs to drop on foes or frail floors and keeping contraptions continuing ladders scarcely impossible.

6. Post for bursting pots

Staying regarding the matter of destruction, you'll need to pay special mind to little pots with a fire. They're by and large kicking around in social events and are your perilous way to new districts. Passages blockaded with wood and red stone can be detonated if you hurl one of these pots their general way. Books of Knowledge are much of the time hidden behind such dividers so pay special mind to pots and you'll generally speaking find a gateway not far away. Recall exorbitantly that if you throw and miss, go for to some degree go around and you'll see that the pot will have respawned to allow you to have another go.

7. Open Advanced Assassination

On the off chance that you're bungling on a stealthier playstyle since AC has indeed presented roughage and murder ropes across streets, the Advanced Assassination ability is critical. It's along the yellow line or, Way of the Raven, on your capacity tree and allows you to execute even critical level enemies if you sort out some way to prevail at a QTE minigame. You ought to just tap the slaughter button once to execute and thereafter tap it again when the marker is in the highlighted zone to fell even the mightiest of enemies. You can even murder likely chiefs before they comprehend what's hit them.

8. Keep your jolts outmaneuvered up

Along these lines, unlike Assassin's Creed Odyssey where it was definitely not hard to walk around with Kassandra outfitted with many blasting and hurt jolts, that is basically not the case this time around. With no jolt making on the fly, you'll need to find them for your bow. That infers looting from racks in camps and houses, and grabbing jolts from dead animals and your murdered adversaries. They can moreover be found standing apart of tree stumps on occasion so look out for your ecological factors regardless, when you're in more provincial zones. They'll be there some spot. Especially if the response for a puzzle or advancement challenge depends after using your bow.

9. Pound pots for loot and snakes

This is just a general feature build up the sheer destructibility of this world. Boxes and mud pots (not the ones referred to before aside from in the event that you instantly need consumed) can be destroyed to grab the loot from inside. They moreover now and again secure openings in the divider that you can slide through to find altogether more loot. Also, sorry Indy, yet from time to time there are creeping stuns concealed in pots. Regardless, at whatever point you've butchered the possessing snake, you can plunder them for snake eggs to hand into your Hunting Hut for extensively all the more shining things.

10. Get treasure swarm maps

If you valued the fortune maps from Black Flag, indisputably so did the dev gathering. Get your hands on a fortune swarm map, appeared by a material marker on your guide and compass, and you'll have the choice to scratch those X indicates the spot needs immediately. There's a fortune swarm map fragment in your pack from your stock screen and a couple of materials display a drawn guide and the locale you'll find the fortune. Various materials will have a letter explaining where the abundance have been concealed. The loot will move yet we've found schematics for longship customization.

11. Put aside some push to flyte

Across Mercia you'll find craftsmen. Versifiers of tongue and don't they know it.

Require some speculation with them nonetheless, pick up capability with your claim to fame, and your appeal bar's not senseless.

Flyting practice gives you charm so contribute your energy and stray from hurt.

12. You can shoot fish (and detonate them)

Aaaand proceeding with common composing PC programs, it's an ideal occasion to shoot some fish. Really, genuinely. While you can clearly, all things considered, fish for fish with your line, if you can see them swimming around you can get them with a jolt if diligence genuinely isn't one of your strong core interests. You can in like manner throw in one of those risky pots if you genuinely need to make some mischief the organic framework.

6 Things the Game Doesn't Tell You

Focus in on Your Settlement First

Near the beginning of Valhalla, Eivor develops their Settlement in the center of England, a shielded haven for their viking clan. The Settlement may seem, by all accounts, to be pretty little from the beginning, with several updates available, yet on the off chance that you're willing to contribute the push to aggregate resources, your Settlement can really uphold Eivor incredibly, opening extra overhauls and detail additions to prosperity, insurance, hurt, and that is only the start.

Mastery Points Really Change the Way You Play

There's a huge load of aptitudes to open and procure in Assassin's Creed Valhalla. Like, a titanic entirety. While by a long shot the vast majority of the capacities open are truly uninvolved, for example, raising your prosperity or passing mischief, there are some that can truly change the way where you play the game.

For example, if you put assets into the gold Assassination Skill Tree, you'll open the ability to cut down two foes immediately with a passing attack. Of course, an aptitude allows you to stomp on the heads of foes in the red Melee Skill Tree, effectively giving you an execution attack. Zero in on the aptitudes you need to open, since they're genuinely going to change Eivor.

Recall that you can transparently reset your capacity centers! Essentially check the base right corner of the screen for the catch to press.

Falcon's Dive Isn't Automatically Unlocked

Alright, the Eagle's Dive. A detailed achievement of marvel when pulled off precisely, and an anomalous thing of catastrophe when the game glitches and your expert assassin goes splat into the ground. It turns out the Eagle's Dive isn't generally opened from the soonest beginning stage of Assassin's Creed Valhalla. To get this component, you need to manufacture the Hidden Ones Bureau, and banter with Hytham, who shows Eivor the techniques for the

Eagle's Dive.

Use Light Bows in Close Combat

Hear us out on this one. There's a subcategory of bows in Assassin's Creed Valhalla called light stops, in a general sense fill in as fast discharging rifles, firing jolts with unfathomable speed without disadvantage time.

Make sure to use light pulls out from fight. They can be really useful for passing on smart damage to a serious adversary, allowing you to get in a lively relatively few shots and bothering them, while in like manner giving you some short an ideal occasion to retouch.

The Cultists Are Back, in a Big Way

Review the Cult of Kosmos from Assassin's Creed Odyssey? Valhalla pits a similar adversary power against Eivor called the Order of the Ancients. There's an entire furnished power out to stop you, with officials, pioneers, lieutenants, to say the least. None of the recently referenced commandants are opened and clear from the most punctual beginning stage of Valhalla, so it's genuinely easy to dismiss them. Assemble the Hidden Ones Bureau in your Settlement if you need to begin pursuing down these shadowy specialists.

Find Vantage Points to Uncover the Blank Map Quicker

Everything in Assassin's Creed Valhalla is more noteworthy than what went before, and that consolidates the game's guide. Exactly when you appear in England, there's a mind-boggling clear manual for uncover, which from the beginning seems like you can simply do by adventuring around as Eivor and examining the entire guide.

A simple course to opening the guide is to find vantage centers. These are meant by a bird of prey on the guide, and at the beginning of the game, they're all white, hailing that they haven't yet been found and synchronized. In the occasion that you've played Assassin's Creed using any and all means, you comprehend what comes immediately: find the vantage point, ascend to its most noteworthy point, and synchronize to open it as a brisk travel point.

It's not just a snappy travel point that you're opening, in any case. Synchronizing with a vantage point will moreover uncover the incorporating guide an area, getting together the fog of war. Doing this will uncover near to reasons for Wealth, depicted with shining gold circles, similarly as side excursions, collectibles, and that is just a hint of something larger.

Professional killer's Creed Valhalla manage: 6 top Valhalla tips you should know

Extra to update your allocates and quiver early

Calfskin and Iron Ore are two of the most notable resources in Valhalla, used generally for updating weapons and protective layer. However, don't scoop them all into better edges and shields straight away. Taking everything into account, save them for working out your allocates and quiver first.

Start with distributes, as each extent consumed gives a tremendous thump in prosperity, so getting three accessible to you early is defended, notwithstanding all the difficulty to lighten avoidable passings in fight. At whatever point you've done that, usage the remainder of develop your quiver. Each jolt is fundamentally a free execute in the early game, and you'll require the extra ammo, as gone weapons like the Recurve Bow start with a measly five shots.

Match your playstyle with your weapons and defensive layer

At whatever point you're fit and flush with ammo, ensure you're not wasting subtlety helps by planning your weapons and shield to your playstyle. The game doesn't explain this well for sure, yet it's extremely huge. Look at the ability tree and see whether the school of the Raven (Stealth), Wolf (Ranged), or Bear (Heavy) takes your lavish, by then check whether you have covering and weapons organizing that school arranged.

In each capacity tree, there are 'Technique for the X' centers that conceivably offer lifts in the event that you're wearing things from your picked playstyle. Covering, at that point, comes in sets that give express awards to wearing every one of the five pieces from a comparable school.

Get each Book of Knowledge in Norway

Expert assassin's Creed Valhalla starts in Norway on an overwhelmingly gigantic landmass stacked with images, yet (spoilers!) you quickly set sail to attack the English coast after the underlying very few story missions. Appearing in England opens a couple of fundamental features including the settlement system, so don't vacillate unreasonably, yet you ought to get each Book of Knowledge in Scandinavia before you leave.

Books of Knowledge give Eivor enduring induction to limits, so you'll require anyway numerous as could be permitted to make fight much less complex when you appear in Britain. There's a spectacular limit I'm really using in the mid-game called Rage of Helheim. You can get this by heading behind the course in the easternmost bit of Rygiafylke. Indication of Death (found in Alkestrad) is in like manner instrumental.

Get Advanced Assassinations to cheddar raised level foes

Likely the best inclination you can get in the early game is called 'Advanced Assassinations', found in the school of the Raven in the lower left of the titanic capacity tree. If you murder raised level enemies without it, you won't execute them completely. However, with Advanced Assassinations opened, an energetic time event will trigger during the kill. In case you nail the QTE, you'll butcher miniboss baddies and other problematic foes immediately, keeping an essential separation from the gibberish of a drawn-out battle. You can utilize this capacity to battle at a shockingly elevated level class in attacks and gain induction to critical level resources and stuff early.

Strike early and attack splendid

At the point when you land in England, you'll set up your camp and start the central questline, zeroing in on areas and clarifying their ability fights. Anyway before you dive into the meat of Assassin's Creed Valhalla, it justifies striking as much as could sensibly be normal, getting the arrangements critical to open huge settlement structures.

Advancement reveals the game's best time features, like Reda's arrangements, Legendary Animals, the Order of the Ancients, to say the very least. You should see a couple of assaults open to you in your close by an area on the guide, a critical number of which may look overpowering from the beginning. Nonetheless, in case your Power level is during the 100s, you should have the alternative to supervise them with key usage of clandestineness and limits. Strikes end when you open up each deftly box at the camp or strict network, so trap and murder the heavy hitters first, by then blow the horn, power the doors open, take your loot, and quickly escape. By then head home and value fleshing out your settlement early.

Change Valhalla into Sekiro

Review the Mikiri Counter from Sekiro? The limit that let you run into an unblockable attack to discredit and counter it? Expert assassin's Creed Valhalla has its own high-peril, high-reward interpretation called the Counter Roll. Far West from the earliest starting point phase of the Raven fitness tree, you'll find this limit that makes the game's unblockable attacks blockable.

At the point when opened, if Eivor runs into an adversary, they will tumble over their back and free by then up to deadly betrays. Exactly when you start encountering Dark Souls-style director fights, where adversaries have colossal prosperity bars and goliath shock quantifies, this inclination gets basic to your perseverance, protecting you from getting scratched by the tip of a spear and desynchronising.

Lead a horse to water

At the point when you have enough supplies from your underlying strikes, your first concern should be to open the Stable just past the Longhouse. This will allow you to purchase mount overhauls from Rowan, one of which is the Horse Swimming update. If you've ever lived in England, you'll know it's a wet spot, anyway this capacity allows your horse to pony through the most significant streams without barely making the slightest effort.

As you would imagine, there's a lot of passing by horseback in Valhalla, and you'll encounter a great deal of conditions where you'd ideally insight over around. Taking everything into account, this inclination is a tremendous trick of the trade: Pick it up as in front of timetable as could be normal the situation being what it is.

Get the Heavy Dual Wield aptitude to transform into a monster

In the northwestern bit of the capacity tree, following the red way of Aspect of Bear aptitudes, you'll find Heavy Dual

Wield, a favorable position that we should you utilize two-gave weapons with just one hand. By and by you can wear twofold Dane Axes, or twofold spears, and these extra mixes are frantically awesome. Besides, two-gave weapons will when all is said in done hit essentially harder than their one-gave accomplices, so you'll achieve more damage too.

Turn up the examination inconvenience to make the game more distinctive

Exploring England is heaps of fun, anyway it's better if you turn off a part of the extreme embellishments that take a huge load of the thought out of wandering around. With the examination inconvenience turned up, things will be all the more genuinely to discover and you'll be given less help (like being shown the detachment to a near to thing). This may sound frustrating, anyway it makes Valhalla generously more clear and fun. As of now, as opposed to feeling like you need to check things of a once-over, you can basically wander around and research at your amusement, and the world is thickly squeezed with enough stuff that sniffing around confusing remaining parts and finding fortune will feel also satisfying and empowering.

Make an effort not to maintain a strategic distance from Flyting challenges

Very quickly, you'll be familiar with Viking rap battles—called Flyting—which fabricates your appeal and unexpectedly opens extra trade decisions. Do whatever it takes not to evade these. Without demolishing anything, there are a couple of events where these extra trade decisions will open up new courses through the story that can be unfathomably important or help diffuse conditions where treasured characters are at serious risk.

Whether or not you're not a craftsman, Flyting is commonly basic. Just guarantee your answer rhymes with your enemy's hold back and passes on a comparable significance. In the occasion that they're examining what a moron you are, the better decision is the one that leaves them rather than switches focuses completely.

Professional killer's Creed Valhalla apprentice's guide: 9 hints for hopeful vikings

PLAY LIKE A VIKING UNTIL YOU CAN PLAY LIKE AN ASSASSIN (AND THEN DO BOTH)

In what's transforming into an example in Assassin's Creed games, you don't start Assassin's Creed Valhalla as an expert assassin. You won't start with the wrist edge or even the ability to slaughter. You won't get the Leap of Faith for a couple of hours (you can regardless ricochet off of things, anyway it's not as smooth).

Slope toward that. Do whatever it takes not to save a second to play as an ax utilizing legend for the underlying very few hours. This is apparently the best movement game in the plan. Mystery isn't required (or even unnecessarily significant), so walk straightforwardly in and hack off heads. Dispatch strikes, and convey your viking bunch into fights with you.

USE ODIN'S SIGHT CONSTANTLY

Odin's Sight is Valhalla's version of Eagle Vision or the Animus Pulse.

Odin's Sight will highlight sustenance (for repairing) and resources (for making gear overhauls). It'll include loot and collectibles regardless, when they're far underground or regardless out of sight.

A huge load of the engaging you do will be experiences between social affairs of equivalently dressed contenders. Odin's Sight will highlight your enemies for you. You can't by chance (or purposely) attack your accomplices, yet knowing which ones are targets will save you an immense heap of time and confusion.

Make setting off Odin's Sight into an inclination any time

you're in a settlement — you don't have to pressure so a ton while out in the focal point of no spot or while you're basically cruising using follow road.

FOLLOW ROAD ON HORSEBACK AND FOLLOW SHORE IN YOUR BOAT ARE WEIRD

While in your longship or riding a pony, you'll have decisions to travel subsequently. There are a few things happening here, notwithstanding, that make it worth taking a breather to explain.

At whatever point you're sunk into your vehicle of choice, you'll get a brief to hold down a catch to come whatever heading you're going up against normally. Riding a pony, this will follow the road. On your boat, this will follow the shore. Without a waypoint, you'll essentially progress forward.

To make an excursion to a waypoint dependent on your own inclination, first set a waypoint on your guide (or clear waypoints and have an excursion followed). Next, start following a road or the shore. By then, when you're moving, you'll get a brief to take off to your checked target. Hit the catch, and you're on autopilot with a target.

WEAPON AND ARMOR QUALITY AND UPGRADES

You won't be drenched with new stuff in Assassin's Creed Valhalla. You'll find a couple, yet for the most part, you'll be remaining with gear for broadened time spans.

The sum of your stuff — weapons and cautious layer — can be upgraded, and updates come in two varieties.

The first is straightforwardly in your Inventory menu. Buoy over a touch of stuff, and you'll see what resources you need to refresh that thing. This is normally commonly iron mineral and calfskin. This sort of update improves your stuff's subtleties.

The other kind of upgrade should be done at a metal counterfeiter's shop. Spending Carbon Ingots upgrades a thing's quality. Each degree of significant worth opens extra update spaces (the upgrades from your Inventory menu), Rune openings (for detail cleaning Runes), and remedial skins. Redesiging a thing's quality doesn't improve its subtleties, be that as it may.

THERE IS A WORLDWIDE ARROW SHORTAGE

If you use your bow a ton (as we do), you will see that jolts are not really plentiful in Assassin's Creed Valhalla. Your bow is as yet extraordinary, so you ought to use it, anyway you should in like manner be set up to require for ammo.

Quest for jolts while ravaging. Odin's Sight will highlight them, and you can generally speaking find jolts where you find foe toxophilite — in pinnacles and cautious stages.

You in like manner get an occasion to accumulate jolts you shot when you loot or even gravitate toward to enemies or animals you've executed. Make it an affinity to check the dead bodies to restock. (Starting late, we had one fastener in our quiver that we kept using for murders and thereafter assembling by and by into our quiver for another manslaughter for around an hour.)

Another quick note about jolts: There are three kinds of jolts to arrange the three kinds of bows, and they are not general. You'll require Hunter Arrows for your Hunter Bow, Predator Arrows for your Predator Bow, and Light Arrows for your Light Bow.

Upgrade YOUR QUIVER AND RATIONS POUCH EARLY

One way around the jolt need is to upgrade your quiver. In your Inventory menu, coast over your quiver, and you'll get a brief to update. Much equivalent to your other stuff (above), you'll use iron metal and calfskin here. Overhauling your quiver will allow you to pass on more electrical discharges (sort).

Basically, straightforwardly underneath your quiver, you'll see your extents pocket. Upgrading this will allow you to pass on different extents — effectively patching blends.

Buy UPGRADE MATERIALS AT SHOPS

You'll find a great deal of materials — unequivocally iron mineral and cowhide as you wander the world. You'll use these ceaselessly to refresh your stuff. Refreshing will require an always expanding number of resources as you continue, and you'll quickly outflank what you're finding.

Shops will sell iron metal and calfskin for 1 silver each, and they generally pass on around 200 of each. You're probably never be low on silver, so get them out every open door you get.

PROPOSED POWER IS IMPORTANT, EXCEPT WHEN IT ISN'T

Territories of Valhalla's existence go with proposed Power levels — capacity centers and stuff upgrades. For the most part, this is a mind boggling reprimand to just stay away from these regions completely. In any case, when it isn't.

Specifically, in Act 1: Battle for the Northern Way segment 4 "Inheritances," you get an objective to "Show up at Alrekstad." (That is a huge load of words to state, enough, "a few hours into the game.") Alrekstad is in Hordaflyke, a domain with a 280 Power proposition — positively some place to dodge when your Power is likely under 10.

For this circumstance, be that as it may, you're totally protected to head there and you need to propel the story. Looking at propelling the story ⋯

Consider PLAYING THE MAIN STORY FOR A (LONG) WHILE BEFORE WANDERING

You need to follow the principal story for a couple of hours before you get to the Assassin's Creed-y part of Assassin's Creed Valhalla. It will likely take you a few hours to attempt to see the title screen.

It appears as though you're delivered into an open world to expert assassin your way through right from the most punctual beginning stage, anyway Assassin's Creed Valhalla has a lot of track to lay. For example, you won't have the alternative to do Sneak Attacks or Assassinations until a piece into Battle for the Northern Way segment 2. You won't have the choice to do the Leap of Faith until the completion of Act 1 (to some degree after you see the title screen).

It's on you to follow the story missions and that is more determinedly than you'd might speculate. There's quite a lot of stuff to do, along these lines a ton to explore, that it's definitely not hard to get redirected. Moreover, you should. Exploring is hugely satisfying and gets you significant prizes (upgrades, aptitude centers, and new stuff, for example).

Our proposition is to coordinate completing all of Act 1 "The Battle for the Northern Way" (the underlying five areas). That will get you to the fittingly Assassin's Creed some segment of the game and open up a huge load of new mechanics. There're a great deal of interferences on the way — you can examine all of Rygjafylke with our aides and you'll venture up a piece, yet your goal should be to finished the principle showing.

TIPS and TRICKS

Zone Scouting and Odin's Sight

If you have played Assassin's Creed Origins or Odyssey, you'll be exceptionally familiar with using a winged creature to scout territories, name enemies, and loot. This is reasonably the comparable in Valhalla, yet with some minor changes. Your Raven, Synin, is so far advantageous for researching regions a respectable decent ways from high questionable. As opposed to using the raven for naming, the repaired view will therefore pull ventures, central focuses, and resources in observe. You can similarly put markers with the raven to help keep with following once you are back on the ground.

Using the raven to scout territories works perfectly with another limit that Eivor has, called Odin's Sight. This is the beat expert that you will use routinely. It will highlight foes and close by critical things that could be of interest. Things, for instance, wealth, keys, side targets, and that is just a glimpse of something larger, are affected.

Viking Combat Tips

The fight in Assassin's Creed Valhalla isn't exorbitantly not equivalent to the past titles, anyway there are discernible changes. If you favor toxophilism in fight, for example, there is by and by a weak point on the adversaries to zero in on. This will wipe out a bit of a state bar over the enemy, called an insurance opening. Forgoing this protect opening is a smart technique to incapacitate them and do impressive mischief simultaneously. A couple of enemies have a singular frail point and some have unique. The weak point will be an astonishing orange spot on the adversary when you center around them with your bow.

You by and by moreover need to deal with a perseverance bar for the fight to come, confining the events you can dodge far eliminated and square with your shield. A couple of players will find this disillusioning, which is sensible. This detail is similarly impacted by the substantialness of your stuff. The heavier your stuff, the more perseverance you will eat up.

Exactly when you are in a condition where you need to evade an extensive sum, don't spam the movement. You will drain the perseverance bar quickly, so time the dodge to the adversary's attack to endeavor to make it as gainful as could be normal the situation being what it is. Your perseverance will empower as time goes on, so if you are low, dial down for a short piece prior to reconnecting the adversary.

Use this methodology for obstructing too. You can hold up your shield anyway long you need, yet the amount of hits you take while obstructing will cause critical harm. If you follow this method, you will similarly end up countering enemy attacks often. The blocking get is equal to repulse and using a second conflict weapon when you are twofold utilizing. Timing a repulse with an ensuing attack will finish the battle quickly.

Making sure about more Abilities

The limits tree in Assassin's Creed Valhalla has been fixed up. You will by and by don't have to spend skill centers to get these limits. They are found the entire path over the land, concealed in things called "Books of Knowledge." These are absolutely discrete from your inclination tree, which gives reserved limits and non-equipable limits. If you need to secure these limits from the "Books of Knowledge," create the Cartographer in your settlement. You can purchase maps for covering and limit zones that will show up on your basic guide.

Step up Eivor

In Assassin's Creed Valhalla, venture up your character has grasped another strategy. It's luckily an immediate course of action that gives a basic strategy to venture up without the steady experience pound. Your levels rely upon the quantity of capacities centers you have apportioned to your character. These centers need to truly be spent in your ability tree and not just remain there as idly.

The skill tree is isolated into three districts for secretiveness, fight, and ran fight. If there is a certain playstyle you like, the capacity tree licenses you to consider the way in which you play. Fighting enemies, striking, insider facts, and side activities all give straightforward ways to deal with get understanding and capacity centers. If you need to have a huge level character, do all that you can on the guide.

Flyting (Rap Battles)

Viking rap battles? That is correct! You can take up challenges against others in Assassin's Creed Valhalla with a verse against abstain rap battle called Flyting. This is a little game that you'll need to pay special mind to in all around arranged towns. Near to the shrewd words that are thrown around, there is a preferred position to participating in Flyting. Your character has a moxy detail that impacts talk choices. The more Flyting battles you win, the higher the allure level. You may be incited on explicit occasions for an extraordinary trade decision, ordinarily offering an elective response for a mission that may not be available something different. Quest for a blue, smiling cover image on the manual for move others to Flyting.

Weapon and Armor upgrades

If you need better, more great stuff and weapons, there are a few things you ought to do. For a certain something, is going out and finding them. There are not a huge load of weapons that can be quickly obtained during Assassin's Creed Valhalla. You should go out, and either get them from a vendor or find them on the planet during your encounters. Here are generally the current defensive layer and weapons levels in Valhalla.

Fine/Gray: Two update base detail spaces.

Unmatched/Bronze: Four upgrade base detail spaces.

Flawless/Silver: Seven upgrade base detail spaces.

Unbelievable/Gold: Ten update base detail spaces.

The higher the level, the harder it is to find the material expected to climb to that level. There is furthermore a second area that can be refreshed on your insurance and weapons, influencing when all is said in done base subtleties. This is segregated from the levels. Exactly when you climb to each new level, it will give additional base detail upgrade openings.

Most will start at a sub-par quality level, either dim or bronze. To refresh, you ought to find the most ideal materials. To move your weapons and covering into more significant levels and augmentation base subtleties, these are such materials you will require.

Cowhide: Commonly found by pursuing and pillaging.

Iron Ore: Commonly discovered all through the guide, keep an eye out for shimmering stores of rocks of obsidian stone.

Surface: An extraordinary material found in chests.

Titanium: An extraordinary material discovered all through the world.

Carbon Ingots: Found in the early domains of England and Norway.

Nickel Ingots: Found in moderate difficulty zones in England, excellent to find.

Tungsten Ingots: Found in high difficulty domains, this material will upgrade defensive layer and weapons to their last level.

In case you decide to start upgrading fortification and a couple of weapons, it's ideal to remain with them for a fair piece of the game until you update something else to an equal level to supersede it. If you spread out your upgrades, you may be more delicate with gear than you should be.

Stick to your top decisions until you find out about open to trading equipment.

Assemble Gear Resources

Valhalla isn't as loot considerable as Odyssey, so you probably won't need to persistently exchange out new weapons and security pieces. Taking everything into account, you'll have a humble bundle of assurance that you can update using resources for improve their subtleties and addition their number of rune openings available. In this way, to exploit your support, be saving watch for resources any place you go. Pursuing animals produces cowhide and sharp regions have rocks that hold metal. You can channel an area for open resources using your expert assassin vision, or get a predominant view (ha!) of resource stores with your crow.

Watch Your Power Level and Use Disguises

Persistently keep an eye out for your current power level and endeavor to stay in regions where you arrange or outperform that number. It's definitely not hard to wander into regions that are well past your level, which are basically harder to get by in as a result of the presence of the relative multitude of more astounding foes. Moreover, a couple of districts are out and out terrible toward Vikings. If you end up in such a zone, put on your cover to blend in and experience unnoticed.

Adjust Your Difficulties

Valhalla incorporates a few different difficulty settings, including one for Exploration and one for Stealth. The Exploration setting chooses how much information appears on your HUD and guide. More irrelevant HUD infers furthermore searching for yourself using trade and natural clues. Pioneer Mode returns from Odyssey, anyway there's a significantly more immaterial structure this time called Pathfinder. You can moreover flip your compass images, and a customized image to show you the closest examination openings. Clandestineness inconvenience changes adversaries' knowledge of your turn of events, and you can turn on a "Guaranteed Assassination" switch for a more excellent Assassin's Creed experience. The game alerts you this isn't the way it is inferred is to be played, regardless. Finally, a fight inconvenience setting also allows you to switch Aim Assist between Partial, Full, Light, and Off.

Orchestrating Your Missions

Your key mission ventures are taken on by talking with Randvi in the longhouse to sort out what are called Conquests; these are long, multi-mission story bends that you can do in any solicitation. It's basic to observe that once you pick a Conquest, you're made sure about until you've completed the aggregate of its connected missions.

Of course, there is Valhalla's new kind of sidequests, which have been retooled and renamed "World Events." These more characteristic, randomized missions don't have a mission tracker yet they're customarily short and needn't bother with a ton of development. These normally give you some light rewards and experience, and when in doubt they're engaging or astounding to a great extent.

You Can Respec Your Skill Points at whatever point

The capacity tree in Valhalla is tremendous and skill centers will as a rule precede since a long time ago it awards two centers for each level-up. It's a wide spreading tree, and not at all like Odyssey, you can respect at whatever point you need to no detriment. Along these lines, you're permitted to examine a fitness tree to take a gander at a segment of its further evolved systems, by then pivot and assess a substitute branch. This reasonably defogs the ability tree, allowing you to see it with more noteworthy clearness whether or not you haven't balanced explicit portions. For a more significant dive into this subject, take a gander at our Skills and Abilities direct.

Turn in Artifacts for Powerful Rewards

Expert assassin's Creed is known for having numerous

knickknacks to accumulate, and Valhalla is the equivalent. You can turn orchestrated by Ancient seals to the Hidden Ones Bureau, which will acquire you earth shattering unlockable limits. The Hidden One Bureaus furthermore uncovers some understanding into the legend of the expert assassins, which is a completely should for all of you durable Assassin's Creed legend fans out there.

Update Your Settlement

At the point when you move past the instructional exercise zone and try to England, there's abundance to do inside your camp. You'll have to arrange fixing your military quarters to make a jomsviking, a remarkable lieutenant that can include others' universes and procure you some coin in the occasion that they're enlisted. You should similarly place assets into the taxidermist with the objective that you can keep prizes from a little pack of irksome animal pursues.

Exactly when you're hanging out at the camp, you should put aside the work to take an interest in flyt, a sort of Viking rap battle, to overhaul your appeal rating. Moreover, on the off chance that you're ever unsure what to do, it never harms to talk with the people in your settlement. Once in a while it energizes you find new accomplices, get secret limits, and even glimmer abrupt conclusions. However, know, people from your settlement can kick the can for good as you progress the story, so create sure to contribute energy with your top picks while you can.

Go Off the Beaten Path

A bit of Valhalla's best secrets and side missions aren't separate on your guide in any way shape or form, whether or not you synchronize a waypoint. Taking everything into account, it underpins examination and following your faculties. In case you open your guide and quest for places of interest, chances are there's something keeping things under control for you there. It might be a secret boss, extraordinary limit, or even a fascinating World Event. Go out and explore the world instead of simply meandering between waypoints; you'll have an unquestionably more unmistakable time.

Make a Feline Friend

There's a cat wandering England who loathes most by far - y'know, considering the way that it's a cat yet venerates cruising the sharp blue. You can find it near the furthest reaches of Oswald's questline, and a while later it will join your longboat when you go assaulting. This doesn't have a particular continuous connection advantage yet is there any valid justification why you wouldn't require a Viking cat?

Survey the legend.

Expert assassin's Creeds are history games, yet then again they're sci-fi games. As much as each segment is an autonomous romp through a specific recorded setting, you'll similarly (overall) need to put some energy in a high level setting including corporate observation, old animals, and the last days. It's bananas. Plan veterans could probably use a lift. Newcomers thoroughly could (indeed, if they need to remain mindful of Valhalla's forefront partitions). We have you covered:

Leave Norway ASAP.

In the occasion that you've followed the pre-release buzz for this game in any way shape or form, you understand that things are set in ninth century England. You might be flabbergasted, by then, to start up the game and end up in lively, exquisite Norway. To the degree game settings go, it's stunning, yet notice this urging: Get thee to England as fast as time grants.

Norway is basically Valhalla's variation of the Hinterlands, from Dragon Age: Inquisition, or early Pandora, from Borderlands 3. At the point when you move away from it, the game opens up wide. You'll open the full broadness of systems, including a rundown of recognizable Templars to slice and a flourishing settlement to step by step consolidate with a totally utilitarian town. Likewise, look: If you're worried about surrendering the chilly region, don't be. Regardless of the way that the ability to do so accommodatingly ignores some plot centers, you can commonly re-appearance of Norway at the press of a catch to tidy up missed collectibles and look at the aurora borealis.

You can climb (almost) everything.

Like Genshin Impact and that one Zelda game everyone says it inappropriately duplicated, you can climb anything in Assassin's Creed Valhalla. In light of everything, almost everything. There are a few unique cases (sheer sheets of ice, for one), anyway the overall reliable rule is this: If you can see it, you can climb it. Furthermore, not in the least like those recently referenced games, there's no vexatious, croissant-framed perseverance bar to stress over.

Climb the Highpoints first.

If it is, notice it absolutely. Exactly when you show up at another area of the guide, your first thing to deal with should be to climb the total of the Highpoints, which are perceived by a falcon framed picture. This will defog a good bit of the guide, revealing the including topography and some focal issues of interest. Among Assassin's Creed veterans, pounding these out is a drive now.

Use your Odin's Sight liberally.

By clicking in the advantage thumbstick, you can authorize your Odin's Sight—basically, Eagle Vision from a part of the past games. This will highlight various things on the planet: enemies as red, treasure as gold, mission objectives as blue, portal keys as, indeed, gateway keys, and so on There's no drawback for authorizing it ceaselessly, so do as such at whatever point you feel lost (or basically need to get a lay of the land). Who knows: You may even turn up something you'd have regardless missed?

Likewise, since an impressive parcel of the enemies wear covering that is practically vague from your accomplices' tunnels, it might be valuable to send Odin's Sight in the glow of fight. That way, you can without a very remarkable stretch make out who the foes are.

Need some silver? Go fishing!

In the event that you're requiring some extra silver to buy more resources or supplies, a respectable strategy to obtain some silver is to go fishing. More noteworthy fish pay out in any event twelve silver coins a pop, and you can hold an immense heap of them right away.

In shops, sell your knickknacks in mass.

Expert assassin's Creed Valhalla continues with the upsetting PC game show of giving you things that are essentially worthless all around other than the way that you can sell them for silver. Genuinely, why do video games keep doing this? Basically show us the money! Luckily, in Valhalla, these knickknacks don't consume any important stock room. It's just an issue of trying to sell them at a shop, which you can do by investigating to the sell menu (right gatekeeper) and holding "Y" (on Xbox). Neglect to suggests you're just leaving silver on the table.

Put assets into your horse.

Quite exactly on schedule into Valhalla, you'll start to encounter corrals. Here you'll find people who can sell you knew horses and ravens. Even more basically, they can sell you upgrades for your horse. These updates aren't luxurious, especially if you try to fish and sell all of your knickknacks. The primary climb to get promptly is empowering your horse to swim. For individuals who played a huge load of Odyssey and Origins, this will be an enormous second. Finally, you can swim your horse over that little stream rather than unloading your pony, swimming alone, and calling it when you show up at the far shore!

Update your distributes first.

As you play, you'll construct a huge load of cowhide and iron, two resources that are used to redesign everything from your bow's quiver to the security on your back. From the beginning, you should disregard all that and put assets into your extents, which will recover you at the press of a catch. At the point when you start hoping to spend surface a third resource on overhauls, you'll have enough extents to keep your prosperity above water (at any rate on Vikingr inconvenience). By then you can focus in on such other stuff.

Take a couple to get back some self-restraint on how weapons work.

Every weapon or piece of defensive layer in Assassin's Creed Valhalla is outstanding. You won't see it deliver from the bodies of dead adversaries or from subjective loot competent barrels. You also can't separate or sell any of this stuff, which takes a breather to get adjusted to. Or then again perhaps, gear sticks with you for good. If you need better more grounded weapons or harder covering, you need to place assets into what you have. Play around with various weapons and shield, see what suits your playstyle, and subsequently dump your resources into it.

Pick an animal for your guarded layer.

No, this has nothing to do with style. It's about substance. In case you look at any piece of stuff in Assassin's Creed

Valhalla, you'll see one of three animal images: a raven, a wolf, or a bear. Your most astute decision is to pick one and stick with it. As you level up, you'll secure nearly nothing, animal changed prizes that thus apply to any stuff with that animal's image. These prizes are minimal a minor compensation to your fundamental chance here, a little lift to evasion there yet they amass as time goes on. Thusly, if you void the sum of your concentrations into the raven section of your fitness web (more on that in a piece), you'll eventually supercharge the sum of your stuff with a raven image.

Set up your protective layer by set.

Support in Valhalla is composed by sets, all of which have two unlockable favorable circumstances, which can do everything from permitting you everything from an extended fundamental occasion to a lift in speed when you're in a troublesome circumstance. If you get ready two pieces of shield from a given set, you'll open that set's first preferred position. Set up every one of the five, and you'll get the ensuing bit of leeway.

You can "conceal" defensive layer.

From time to time, you find a touch of stuff that is just unnecessarily adequate not to plan. A portion of the time, it's unpleasant. In those models, basically skim over a particular piece of stuff and hold down the advantage thumbstick. That will hide it from sight (yet not from mind, as you'll really collect its sweet, sweet detail benefits).

You can simply guarantee a one zone right away.

Expert assassin's Creed Valhalla had questlines that are appended to various areas. At the point when you show up at England, you'll be incited with a movement of districts to "pledge" to. This will start a multi-segment questline for that region. You can regardless go any spot you need, anyway you can simply complete mainline missions for that district. Additionally, in the event that you're pledged to a one region (state, Ledecestrescire) yet endeavor to promise another (state, Grantebridgescire), you'll be gated off from the Ledecestrescire questline (until you pledge again). Your sharpest decision is to go spaces one by one, seeing each to the end before vowing to another.

Guarantee to Grantebridgescire first.

Exactly when you're at first familiar with the vowing system, just two are inside your ability level: Grantebridgescire and Ledecestrescire. Do the Grantebridgescire questline first. It's not actually as drawn out as the Ledecestrescire one, and encountering it will give you a hold on the way questlines work in this game all the speedier. Prize: You will meet the most manager character in the game sooner rather than later. (Expressions of remorse, no spoilers on this one!)

Do whatever it takes not to capitulate to the open-world walk.

Valhalla's world is colossal, genuinely, and yet it's alive. Pull up the guide, and you'll see gold, white, and blue circles all over. The gold circles infer treasure: ingots (used for improving your stuff), limits (ground-breaking fight capacities), and stuff (unequivocally what it appears as). White circles also mark collectibles, anyway they're not as fast accommodating as the gold fortunes. Both gold and white fortunes regularly require disentangling a sort of basic characteristic conundrum.

The blue circles are also captivating. Gigantic quantities of them are asserted "world events," brief one-acts that grant you some experience centers or what some other game would call a side-mission. Moreover, the vignettes are as often as possible marvelous. (One, in Grantebridgescire, has you delivered an army of cats on an irksome field of rodents.) Some are fascinating more modest than anticipated games, including, yet not limited to, a material science based, stone-stacking game that is abnormally trying; a movement of platforming tests that rival the bouncing a great deal of Assassin's Creed: Revelations; and some Ubisoft-basic pipedream challenges that, to use a particular term, make Eivor trip balls.

This picture means an "Malevolence Anomaly." If you see one, for a conundrum platforming challenge.

Despite where you are, there's no insufficiency of uncommon exercises, so this may sound irrational: Don't focus an extreme measure of time putting forth a unique attempt to hit everything. The questlines you promise will cause them to traipse wherever on the district. As you progress through the segments of each area, hit the subordinate stuff that you come very near. You'll get a great deal of advantages— including the best prize, that of experiencing this brilliantly recognized open world on the way.

Arrange finding Books of Knowledge.

You can slice up most foes with a good ax or sharp edge, anyway it's reliably splendid to have more fight options, so be saving watch for splendid book images on your guide or in-game compass. Get-together these will open new fight limits, some of which are uncommonly important, like one that allows you to shoot twelve jolts at a great deal of targets. Likewise, when you have some incredible limits, keep looking for books, since you can occasionally find an upgrade for limits you starting at now have, making them amazingly better and even more noteworthy.

Fortune aides can show you what to pursue for.

After you build a shack for Ravensthorpe's guide producer,

you'll have the choice to purchase treasure maps. Forking over silver for each one will pinpoint accurately where certain fortunes are, by transforming one of the gold circles on your guide into a successfully conspicuous image. Thusly, if you buy, say, a fortune map for a Book of Knowledge in Oxene for dscire, one of the gold circles on your guide in Oxene for dscire will change into a Book of Knowledge image. The idea here is to use these advisers for limit which circles merit finding (and filtering through which aren't).

Just by looking at these commitments, you'll find that you have five pieces of stuff to get together in East Anglia.

The casual and penny-pressing—procedure here, clearly, is to look at the guide creator's items and use that as an estimation. Assume the guide creator has three limit book images accessible to be bought in Oxenefordscire. You could buy all of them three for 150 silver, at 50 a pop. Or on the other hand you could just use that data to understand that three Books of Knowledge are still wherever in the locale, head over, and do some spelunking exemplary way.

Flyt everyone.

Flyting is, to take it from Atlas Obscura, the old forte of "verbal jousting." It's an enormous bit of Valhalla. As you examine the world, you'll go over various people who need to flyt you. (They're addressed by a camouflage like cover picture.) These little games may seem, by all accounts, to be silly, anyway they offer serious focal points. For one, emerging victorious will get you silver; the more you bet, the more you'll obtain. For another, you'll similarly get a lift to your persona detail. Get your attraction adequately high, and you may even open trade choices that license you to skirt troublesome tasks by, um, "engaging" people to see your course, Fallout-style.

Prize tip: With each round of flyting, you can rapidly limit one of the choices. You will likely pick the articulation that the two matches the musicality to the previous articulation and terminations in an ideal rhyme. Only two of three choices will have that ideal rhyme. Negligence the one that doesn't.

You can skip trade.

Press "B" (on Xbox). It skips by the sentence, not the conversation. Essentially don't do this in a flyt-off, or you'll miss the beat!

Focus in on revealing the total of your capacities.

The inclination tree in Valhalla is more like a mastery spiderweb, with enormous heaps of extending and interconnecting capacities and limits concealed inside. Thing is, you can't see most of it close to the start. As you get capacity centers, endeavor to open aptitudes that have affiliations that go off into the fog past. These will open new aptitudes to... open. The gigantic piece of room here is that you can plan and get accommodating capacities sooner. Do whatever it takes not to worry about getting a mastery you don't enjoy just to open up another portion either, in light of the fact that you can just respec later.

You can respec without repercussion.

Expert assassin's Creed Valhalla doesn't have any respec tokens or require a little fortune of in-game money to rearrange your character. You can reset the whole of your aptitudes, at whatever point, by opening up your mastery web and crushing Y (on Xbox). Regardless, if you would incline toward not to encounter the trouble of reallocating most of your aptitudes essentially correctly where they were, you can reset capacities piecemeal. Just buoy over the one you need to limit and hold X.

Do whatever it takes not to get the Explosive Corpse aptitude.

As you balance your skill tree, you may see some unpredictable aptitudes and think, "Sure, I'll get that, why not?" And that is certifiably not a terrible system in Valhalla, as most capacities are useful or conceivably not meddlesome. Regardless, there is an exception: Don't get Explosive Corpse, a skill that grants you to set catches on bodies. On a fundamental level, it sounds important, anyway eventually it sucks and that is an immediate consequence of the controls. Planning a catch is straightforward: Just hold the advantage thumbstick for fairly near a body. This is moreover a comparative strategy to impel your Odin's Sight. This becomes disturbing when you are enclosed by corpses, which happens an extraordinary arrangement in this game, as you'll go to channel the atmosphere, and a short time later end up bowing near a body for significant whole seconds.

Blasted structures by and large repeat comparable natural enigmas.

Assume an excursion objective or a fortune is rushed behind a passage or is stuck inside some structure with a restricted gateway. How might you get it? For sure, by and large, structures that are made sure about close have a few ways to deal with get in that the game uses over and over. Here are the most broadly perceived and what you should be looking for if you slow down out.

Darted portals: Find the key. Use your Odin's Sight to pinpoint it. It's regularly close by—now and again on a watchman or in a room some spot.

Ousted passages: Look around and check whether there's any window or opening that might be too little to even think about evening consider moving through, anyway might be ideal for shooting a jolt through to break whatever is holding the gateway shut.

Disguised openings: Break any cases or cases that are near the zone you are endeavoring to enter, as habitually little openings that you can slide through will be sought shelter behind these. If not, boxes routinely contain silver so it's a no-lose situation.

Slight and unstable dividers: If you see a divider that takes after it's made out of twigs, it's conceivable delicate. You can by and large check by directing your bow at a divider or door toward see. If your reticle turns red, you can break it! (Furthermore, if you see a wooden board on the floor, shoot it and you can tear it open and go underground and suspect that disturbing fortune you can't get to.)

Use Your Navigation Tools

Like Senu and Ikaros already, Eivor's raven Synin is a huge accomplice who gives a (demanding) 10,000 foot viewpoint on the ground underneath. Nevertheless, unlike the winged partners of past games, Synin's rule quality is in finding motivations behind interests for Eivor to look at while exploring the guide. In spite of the way that she isn't as capable at highlighting foes, the raven is only one of various supportive course instruments accessible to Eivor. Falcon Vision moreover makes a re-appearance of the course of action in Assassin's Creed Valhalla, and it's a fundamental inclination to use while examining a zone for huge things and secrets. Finally, the compass will direct the player toward huge updates like weapons and phenomenal limits. With an expansive guide stacked up with things to discover, do, and explore, it's fundamental to use these instruments to get to huge things.

Quest for Weapons

Constancy is key when looking out new weapons in Assassin's Creed Valhalla, since you should discover them isolated. Weapons won't be aggregated by basically looting enemies; taking everything into account, you'll need to use your navigational gadgets to discover them at unequivocal territories on the guide - making it extensively more basic to sort out examination while on your triumph. There are similarly unfathomable things and weapons holding on to be found, so don't feel like you need to remain with the main weapon you get!

Contribute Energy Building Your Settlement

The Settlement is essentially the middle point for a huge bit of Eivor's encounters. Zero in on stirring up your Settlement. Assault for arrangements to make and update countless the various structures in your Settlement, and contribute energy speaking with your neighbors and accepting the unique compensations of having a strong organization. There are various record bends, missions, activities, and game mechanics accessible through creation and upgrading your Settlement, so it's basic to focus in on developing it to profit by the game.

Recall Your Raiding Party

Everyone understands a Viking is simply on a standard with their assaulting social affair, and it's especially clear in Assassin's Creed Valhalla. To profit by your strikes, you'll need a solid gathering of pirates to help you with opening certain doors and chests, fight foes, and savage force your way through conflict. When stirring up your Settlement, you can change your hoodlums into a destructive force fit for cutting down even the most animated of England's domains. Zero in on them in battle, too; in case they get brought down in a fight, they'll need Eivor to reestablish them and get them in a decent spot once more.

Endeavor Special Abilities

While new aptitudes and capacities are opened by methods for the development structure in Assassin's Creed Valhalla, there are moreover unprecedented limits available to Eivor that think about remarkable focal points all through fight.

Like weapons, these should be found in the open world. You'll consider them to be books, and your compass will help oversee you to them while you're examining.

Put on the raven's outfit ensuing to pounding Rikiwulf

Rikiwulf is the foremost essential chief of the game and the experience with him is portrayed in the part named Bosses. After you oversee Rikiwulf you will get the raven family things and it is worth set them up OK away. This will extend Eivor's base subtleties, as he/she didn't have any novel articles of clothing things subsequent to starting the game. It is moreover worthy to improve all of the things you wear reliably, especially as it will probably require some venture before you start finding or getting other huge outfits.

An additional inspiration to wear segments of the raven's outfit is the prize gotten for wearing things from a comparable set (the shield additional augmentations with the deficiency of prosperity centers and a more noticeable chance of fundamental hits). From the outset you get 4 out of 5 pieces of raven's outfit. The "missing" fifth part is a cap you get as a pay for vanquishing the ensuing essential boss – Kjotve.

Endeavor to show up at Power 20 going before going to England

As an update, Power is a factor showing how strong the holy person is. You can grow this limit overwhelmingly by refreshing your character to the accompanying experience levels and selecting the got capacity centers to open new aptitudes from the improvement tree. Entering a district with too notable enemies suggests significant issues - adversaries will be all the more difficult to survive and will do deal essentially more mischief.

Endeavor to show up at Power 20 going before you leave Norway and go to England startlingly. The underlying two regions in England are recommended for Power 20 characters. You can achieve this motivating force by completing essential excursions just as side activities, for instance, events or finding advantaged bits of knowledge during the primary hours of the game. You will find more information about the portrayed mechanics on an alternate page Suggested Power for a Region.

Use Odin's Sight to discover enemies, keys and fortunes

Eivor can use Odin's Sight from the most punctual beginning stage of the game and it isn't limited in any way. The phenomenal vision mode turns around separating the atmosphere for captivating things. Above all, Odin's Sight can be significant to you for:

Zeroing in on your enemies – this grants you to avoid them even more viably or attack them clueless.

Finding treasure – if you don't see the fortune regardless of the pictures on the guide (for instance the yellow spot) move the camera vertically – it will in general be on the highest point of a structure or under the ground.

Finding the keys – they may lying in plain view or be passed on by enemies. Keys are useful for opening closed passages and cases.

Re-appearance of Gunnar with the found ingots

Gunnar is a very much arranged smithy – during your stay in Norway you can find him in the town of Fornburg, and ensuing to moving to England you will be given the necessary mission of building a cabin for him in the as of late settled Viking settlement. Gunnar has the stuff to improve the idea of Eivor's things, which fabricates their most prominent number of redesigns and allows them to "present" runes.

Keep returning to Gunnar with the ingots found in the game world, as they are used to "cash" gear redesigns (and not silver). Regardless, you should take note of that ingots come in three varieties. Their basic variety - Carbon Ingot - will simply allow the redesign of solid things to amazing. In case you need to make further quality overhauls, you need to find more surprising ingots. For more information, you should see the page Improving your stuff.

Events license you to build a lot of XP

During the game, you can make sure about experience centers in various habits, with World Events being the second-best xp source after missions. We unequivocally endorse that you keep awake with the most recent with all the events found on the world guide, similarly as successfully search for new ones (they may stow away under the blue bits on the guide).

Events are different kinds of little excursions - you may, for example, be drawn nearer to assist with completing a particular activity, to encourage a conflict, or to find something missing. They are neither problematic nor long. The game distinctions you with at any rate 1200xp for completing the event and especially in the fundamental time of the mission it can allow you to show up at higher experience levels extensively more routinely. Zones of events can be found in our world guide book. We also depicted them in the walkthrough direct.

Use the hood to diminish the threat of revelation

Eivor can put on the hood resulting to picking it beginning from the drop menu (the lower heading key on the pad), anyway this is simply possible if the holy person is starting at now not fighting with anyone. The hood is significant in "orange" zones, for instance zones where foes can attack Eivor after he gravitates toward to them. It has two essential applications for sneaking around more effectively and staying concealed:

The hood can concede the acknowledgment of Eivor. This is a significant component, anyway realize that it doesn't guarantee "theoreticalness". It is so far significant while avoiding adversaries at a medium division.

The hood may allow blending in with the ecological elements. For example, Eivor can sit on a seat or stop at a table allowing him/her to conceal. For this circumstance, you don't have to worry about keeping a secured detachment, anyway the impairment of this course of action is the need to stay still. Thusly, this is transcendently useful in case you are keeping things under control for a mission goal or some other event.

Use the materials for the essential updates of allots and quiver.

In the game, you can spend making materials to improve your stock. Before you decide to improve your weaponry and defensive layer, make two distinctive purchases from your stock:

Improve your Rations by consuming 50 pieces of calfskin and 100 iron metals. This will assemble the amount of possible courses of action and likely prescriptions by 1. You will, clearly, believe that its significant during each irksome battle. Another allots update is tragically impressively more exorbitant (140 pieces of cowhide, 300 iron minerals) and it's more intelligent to hold on with it.

Improve the quiver by consuming 30 pieces of calfskin and 20 iron metals. You can in like manner open another level for 80 pieces of cowhide and 50 iron metals promptly or before long. Upgrading the quiver will allow you to pass on more darts in your stock. This will decrease the risk of crippling them during fights and you will less consistently have to find places in the game presence where you can recharge your jolt deftly.

Attempt to quickly erect critical structures quickly in the settlement

Gunnar's smithy lodge is the fundamental structure in the settlement that should be raised. You have a choice with respect to whether to manufacture various structures yet you should think about the way that you will have a very limited stockpile of making materials. Appropriately, it is basic to at first erect structures that will open critical new game mechanics, excursions, and features. Our recommendations are:

(What could be contrasted with the Knights Templar). You will have the choice to perceive the people from the Order and pursue for them.

Military fenced in area – Unlock the opportunity of choosing jomsvikings. You can enroll other players' Vikings similarly as license various players to use your subordinates and bit of leeway from it (you should play on the web).

Tracker's Hut – Unlocks the ability to pass on astounding animal prizes and opens pursuing assignments, which can be compensated with ingots and runes.

Striking the orders grants you to get phenomenal materials

To bring the structures recorded up in the past portion (and all others in the settlement), you must have unprecedented materials. Unfortunately, you will never have any excess of them. The most unsafe are Raw Materials, as they are not found in tremendous sums during a fundamental examination of the game world.

Endeavor to arrange assaults on the cloisters found on the world guide. In each such territory, you will find at any rate two gigantic compartments covering unrefined materials. Attacking strict networks will essentially make it more straightforward for you to raise several starting structures that don't yet require especially a great deal of unrefined materials (a typical of 30-45 materials for each structure).

There are critical choices in the game anyway there are not many of them

Expert assassin's Creed Valhalla, like AC Odyssey and AC Origins, draws inspiration from RPGs and this suggests, notwithstanding different things, that in specific missions you will make problematic decisions. A couple of decisions just barely change the course of a mission or a lone conversation, anyway there are in like manner huge choices in the game that have long stretch outcomes. Your decision may, for example, lead to the acquiring or loss of a potential accomplice, similarly as add to opening another completion of the game.

It is ideal to save the game before each conversation (you can make both manual and rapid recuperations) if there ought to emerge an event of uncalled-for lead or overall picking "some unsuitable" talk elective. Huge choices are portrayed in more detail in the FAQ region and are moreover associated with our walkthrough oversee.

Use the horn to call your partners for help

From the soonest beginning stage of the game, Eivor has a horn that has two applications - it might be used to bring boats and to assemble group people. In the two cases, to use the horn, you need to hold down the lower course key on the pad and select the fitting thing beginning from the drop menu.

The ensuing decision is more useful. Duringyour stay in an undermining zone you can assemble various Vikings to help. This is particularly valuable in conditions where you have failed with the mystery approach and have been recognized, as you won't have to fight all your enemy's isolated from every other person. Regardless, Viking sponsorship can moreover be useful when you need to ensure about a zone faster. In a get-together you can discard enemies even more with no issue.

Quest for the Books of Knowledge

Despite opening new aptitudes you can moreover use dynamic limits. These are momentous fight strategies including the use of engagement and went weapons. With limits you can, notwithstanding different things, shoot hails of jolts, throw hatchets, and charge at foes. As limits are notable attacks their usage is confined - you need to fill the exceptional adrenaline bar.

The most ideal approach to open the new limit is to find the associated book of data - they are one of the collectibles type in the game. After you have taken in the limit, you should add it to the backup way to go bar - Eivor can have 4 run and 4 fight limits arranged at the same time.

HINT& TIPS

Not under any condition like past Assassin's Creed games, most collectible things and central focuses are part into three classes: Wealth (ingots, limits, and weapons), Mysteries (side missions and enigmas or troubles), and Artifacts (cosmetics and fortune maps)

Your raven doesn't reveal enemy territories and therefore mark them as red like winged creatures did in past Assassins Creed games. You can, regardless, actually mark spots while flying as a raven to make finding them as Eivor more straightforward. Note that an early inclination in the Wolf Tree can moreover make perceiving foes easier.

Various doors are ousted on one side - use Odin Sense to recognize the red bars on the contrary side. This normally suggests there's a substitute section – either through the windows, a delicate housetop, or underground. A couple of barricades can even be pounded by slaughtering through breaks in the dividers.

You're likely going to find a huge load of made sure about portals your developments (these won't have red barricades on the opposite side) – anyway keys should reliably be close by. Your raven can recognize if a particular adversary is passing on a key – in case you can't recognize one, it might be the remuneration of a near to World Event.

To loot Wealth during an attack, you'll routinely require a gathering mate to help you either bust down a passage that prompts Wealth or to truly open a chest with Wealth inside. This infers two things: you'll need to shield your gathering mates to keep them alive (and revive them when they go down) and you'll need to clear the foes in a zone near Wealth so your partners can assist you with getting the Wealth.

Not all plenitude like supplies are found at striking targets – more unassuming totals can be found in little chests that appear as tiny gold spots on the guide. These don't count to the collectible plenitude all out of an area, anyway merit social affair to help upgrade your stuff and your settlement.

In the event that you're low on prosperity in fight and out of Rations, circumvented the zone you're doing combating in to find berries or various sustenances in the district to restore your prosperity. After you've restored your prosperity, any food assembled will count toward your Rations meter.

All through the world, you'll find dividers that can be broken. If there's a near to red pot, shoot it with a jolt to cause an impact that in a perfect world destroys the sensitive divider. If you can't find any, you can moreover have a go at using the Incendiary Powder Trap limit if you've opened it, which fires risky jolts. Use this limit on the divider to annihilate it.

The capacity tree is really astounding and you may not for the most part comprehend what you're stretching out towards. Luckily, you can reset the entire tree or a singular point at whatever point to change it up. See the totally uncovered Skill Tree and fitness depictions here!

The more you expand your fitness tree, the more plausible you are to placed assets into capacities that extension the properties of stuff of a specific kind. Advantage from these upgrades by having your stuff acclaim your aptitudes and endeavor to set up a single sort – the Bear, the Wolf, or the Raven.

Eivor won't have a ton of combination fighting in any case – arrange looking out Books of Knowledge to learn limits that usage Adrenaline, and open central Skills in the Skill Tree for focal points that needn't bother with Adrenaline using any and all means.

Eivor has a blue meter that means their perseverance, anyway it doesn't work an astounding way you think. You can regardless run along without getting depleted, anyway kept dodging, holding block, or delivering weighty strikes or easygoing attacks will cut down your perseverance. Losing all your perseverance can make avoiding attacks all the more eagerly, so acknowledge when to stop crushing the attack and back off before you get caught by a counter-attack.

Refreshing your Settlement isn't just for looks – you'll have the choice to open new missions and features subsequently. A couple of things you find like animal parts or roman doodads can't be traded until you've built up the right spots.

While you end up leaving Norway from the earliest starting point in the story, you can truly return at whatever point by hitting the Atlas button on the planet map.

If you see an image for a secret passage on your guide, reliably take a gander at them, as they consistently lead to adore you can't reach regularly. If your raven perceives something under the ground that you can't reach – secret paths are likely the spot to get in touch with them.

You can call your longship to you at whatever point to the

extent that you're near water — hold down on the d-pad and select it on your wheel using the right stick. This is useful for smart, watery departures and when you've left your boat far from your back and forth movement region.

You can check various things on your guide. This is especially useful when you notice that while on the way to a mission, there are distinctive central focuses like a Wealth territory or a World Event.

Just one out of each odd point of convergence will appear on your guide just by synchronizing on a high view point. Some should be uncovered by exploring or tending to wandering information agent NPCs who have a? Over their heads and paying to reveal what a spot on the guide's real prize.

Central focuses consistently pack around greater houses you can strike, or towns you can visit. Once in a while, a town will give new world events or minigames after you've helped accomplices in the area take it over.

Whether or not you're by and large force level doesn't show up at the heights of a neighboring territory, you can even now research them - basically don't wander into any enemy camps.

Adversaries come in different sorts across Valhalla from Saxons to Danes to undesirable religion contenders. Not only will they shake different weapons, they'll use them uniquely, like a spearman driving a profound attack charge, or a viking exchanging from a two-offered ax to twofold hammers. As you experience new enemy types, acknowledge which moves they are good for using to acknowledge when to dodge and when to hold quick and repulse a couple of strikes in progression.

Fire can hurt a ton in case you're not foreseeing it. Douse it quickly by holding the dodge catch to play out a roll.

Every enemy has a run weak point, shown by an orange spot while zeroing in on them with a bow. This can help you with penetrating the gatekeepers of particularly extreme foes, as it will routinely make them defenseless against deaden attacks.